STAR WARS

CLONE WARS

ADVENTURES

VOLUME 1

designer
Darin Fabrick

associate editor
Jeremy Barlow

editor
Randy Stradley

publisher
Mike Richardson

special thanks to Sue Rostoni and Amy Gary
at Lucas Licensing

The events in this story take place approximately
five months after the Battle of Geonosis.

4 6 8 10 9 7 5 3

www.titanbooks.com
www.starwars.com

STAR WARS: CLONE WARS ADVENTURES volume 1, July 2004. Published by Titan Books,
a division of Titan Publishing Group Ltd., 144 Southwark Street, London SE1 0UP.
Star Wars © 2004 Lucasfilm Ltd. & ™. All rights reserved. Used under authorization.

STAR WARS

CLONE WARS
ADVENTURES
VOLUME 1

"BLIND FORCE"
script **Haden Blackman**
art and colors **Ben Caldwell**

"HEAVY METAL JEDI"
script **Haden Blackman**
art **The Fillbach Brothers**
colors **SnoCone Studios, Ltd.**

"FIERCE CURRENTS"
script **Haden Blackman**
art **The Fillbach Brothers**
colors **SnoCone Studios, Ltd.**

lettering
Michael David Thomas

cover
Ben Caldwell

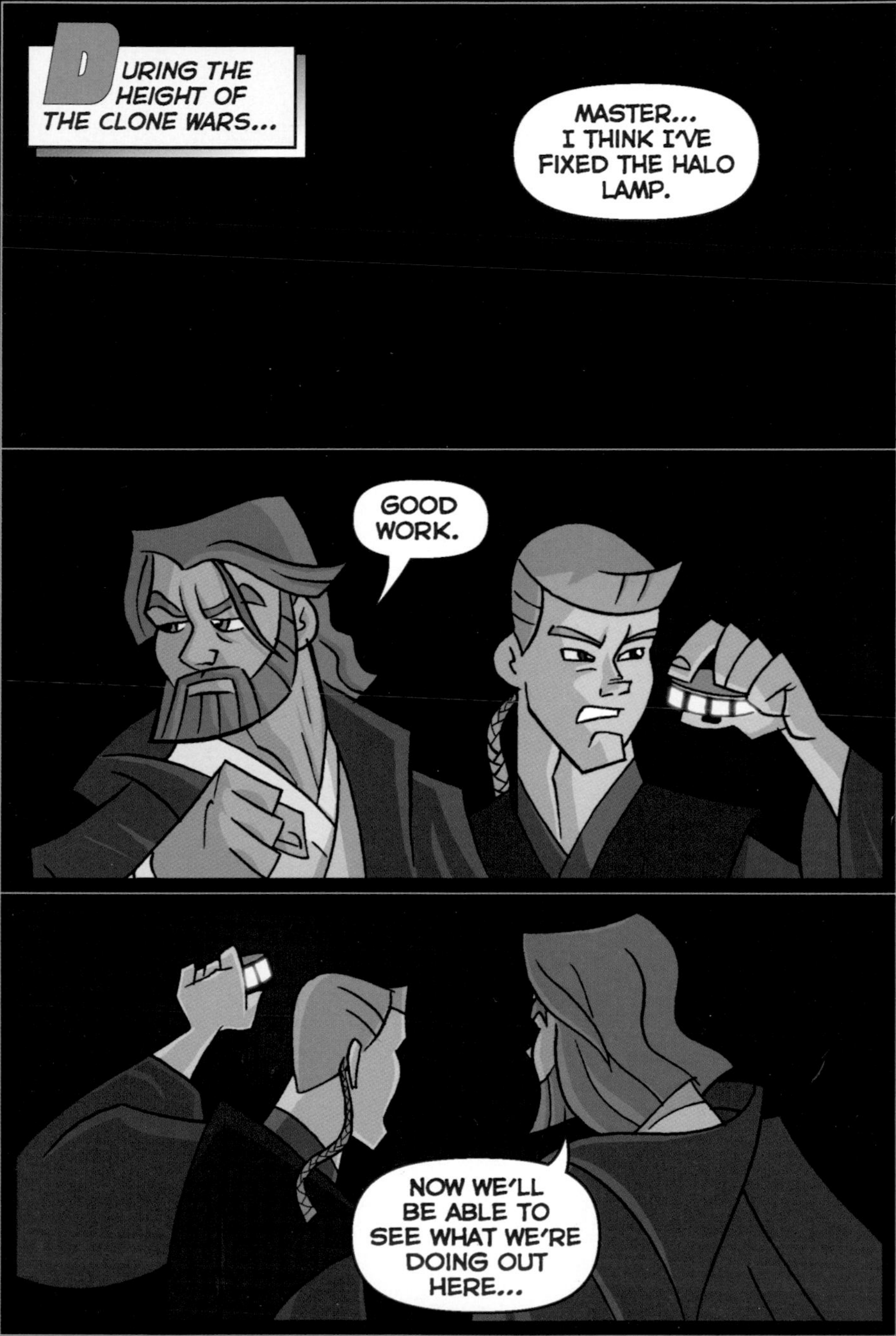
DURING THE HEIGHT OF THE CLONE WARS...
MASTER... I THINK I'VE FIXED THE HALO LAMP.
GOOD WORK.
NOW WE'LL BE ABLE TO SEE WHAT WE'RE DOING OUT HERE...

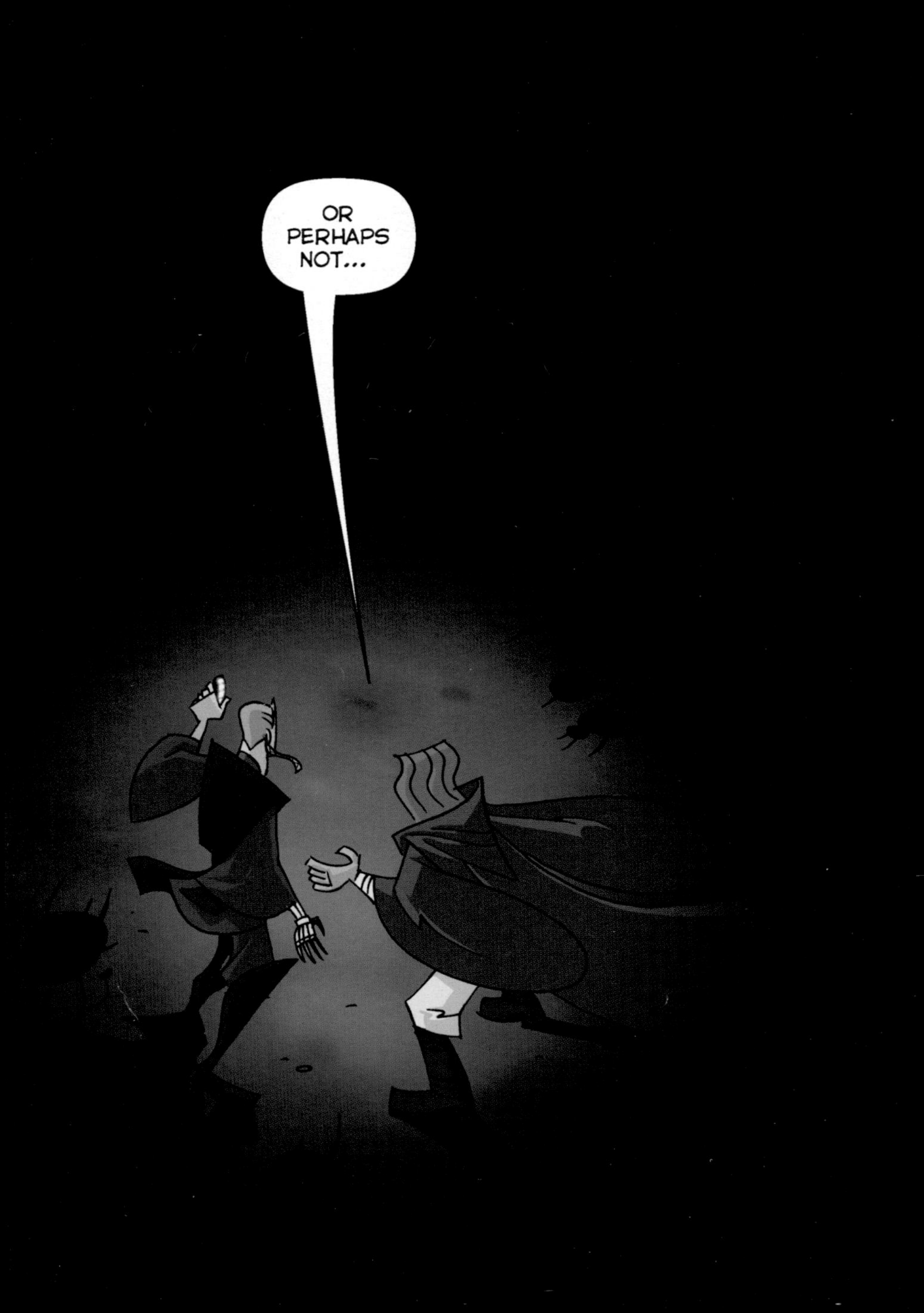
OR PERHAPS NOT...

OBI-WAN KENOBI AND
ANAKIN SKYWALKER IN:

A CLONE WARS ADVENTURE

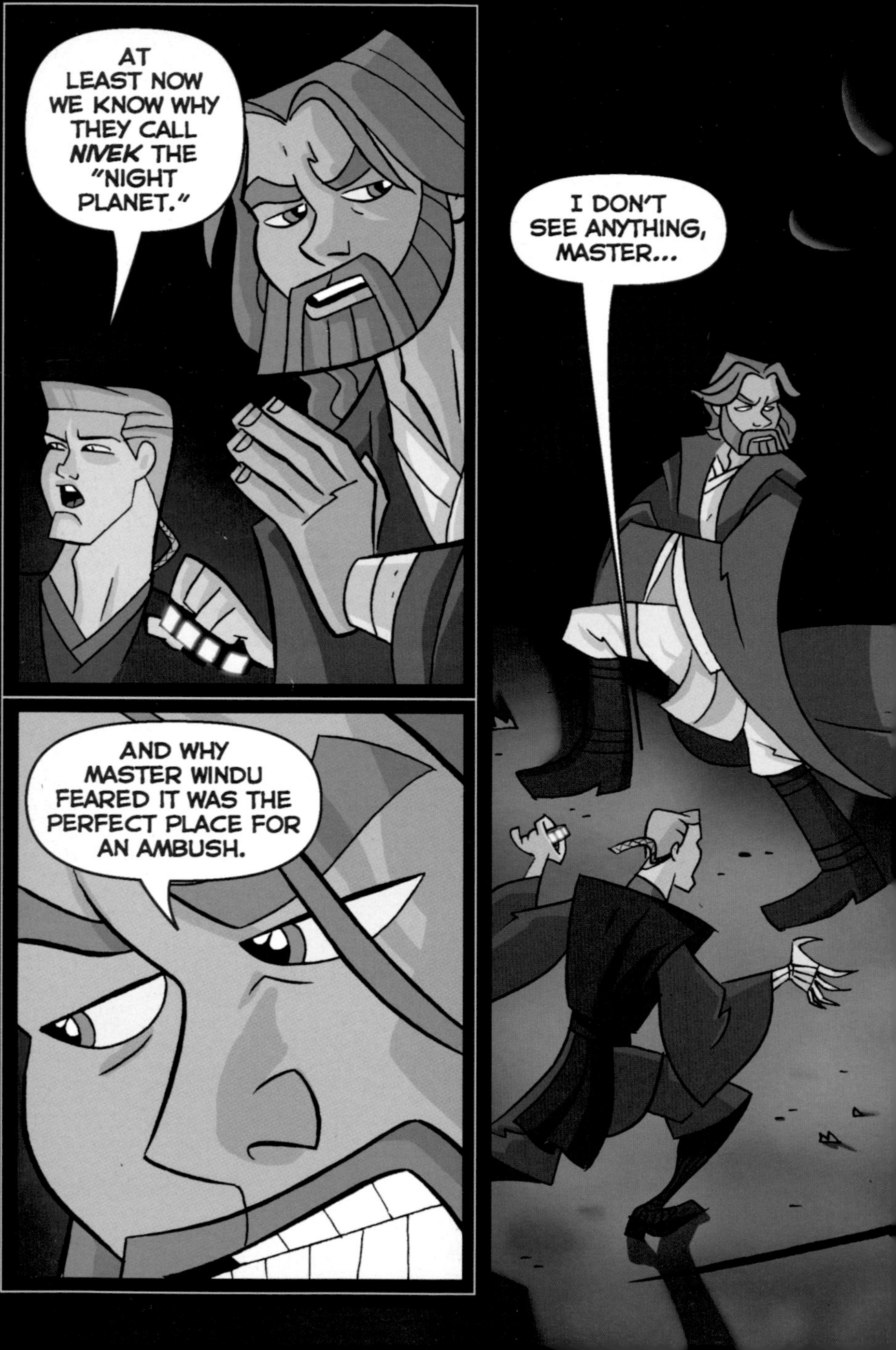
AT LEAST NOW WE KNOW WHY THEY CALL *NIVEK* THE "NIGHT PLANET."
AND WHY MASTER WINDU FEARED IT WAS THE PERFECT PLACE FOR AN AMBUSH.
I DON'T SEE ANYTHING, MASTER...

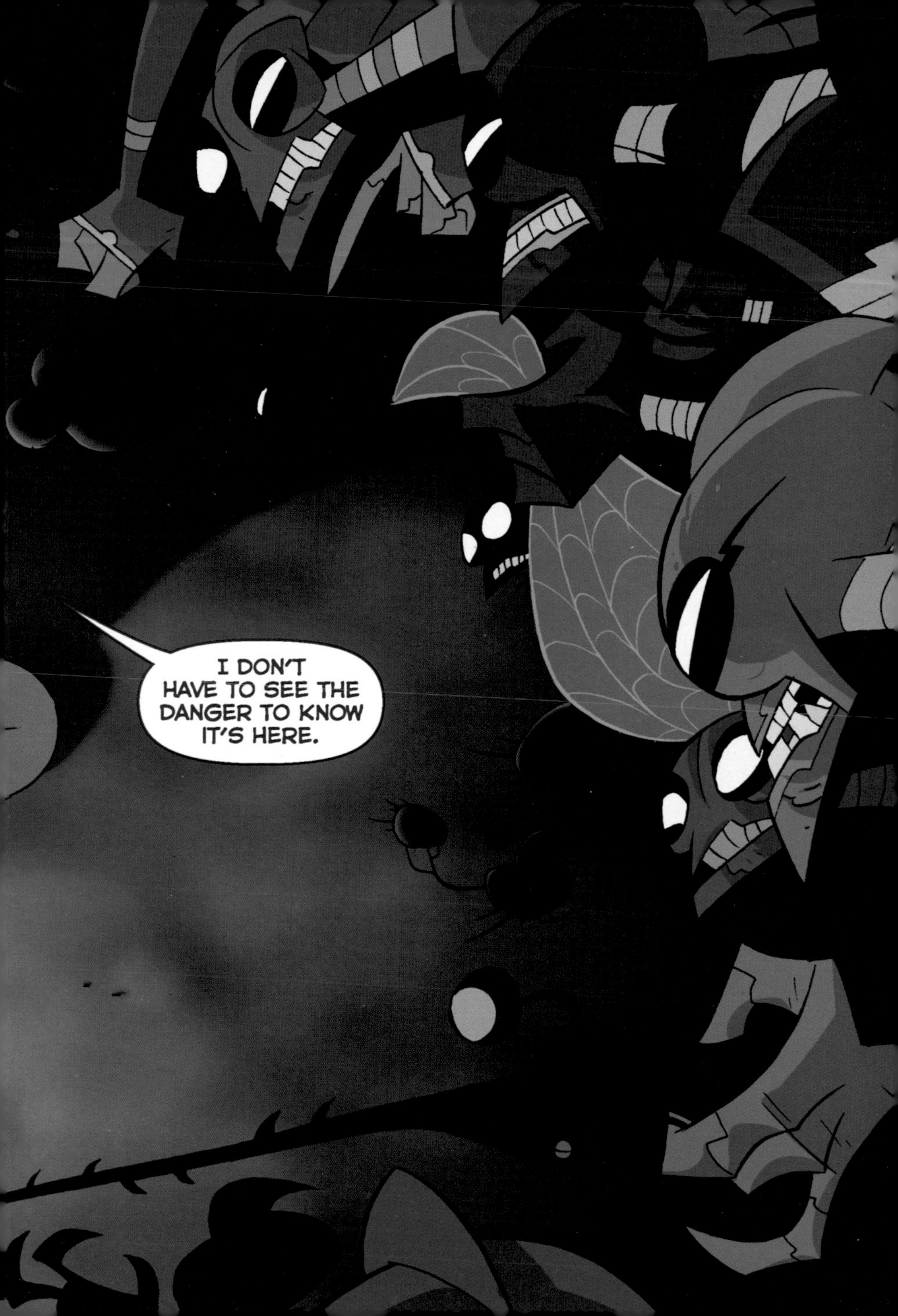
I DON'T HAVE TO SEE THE DANGER TO KNOW IT'S HERE.

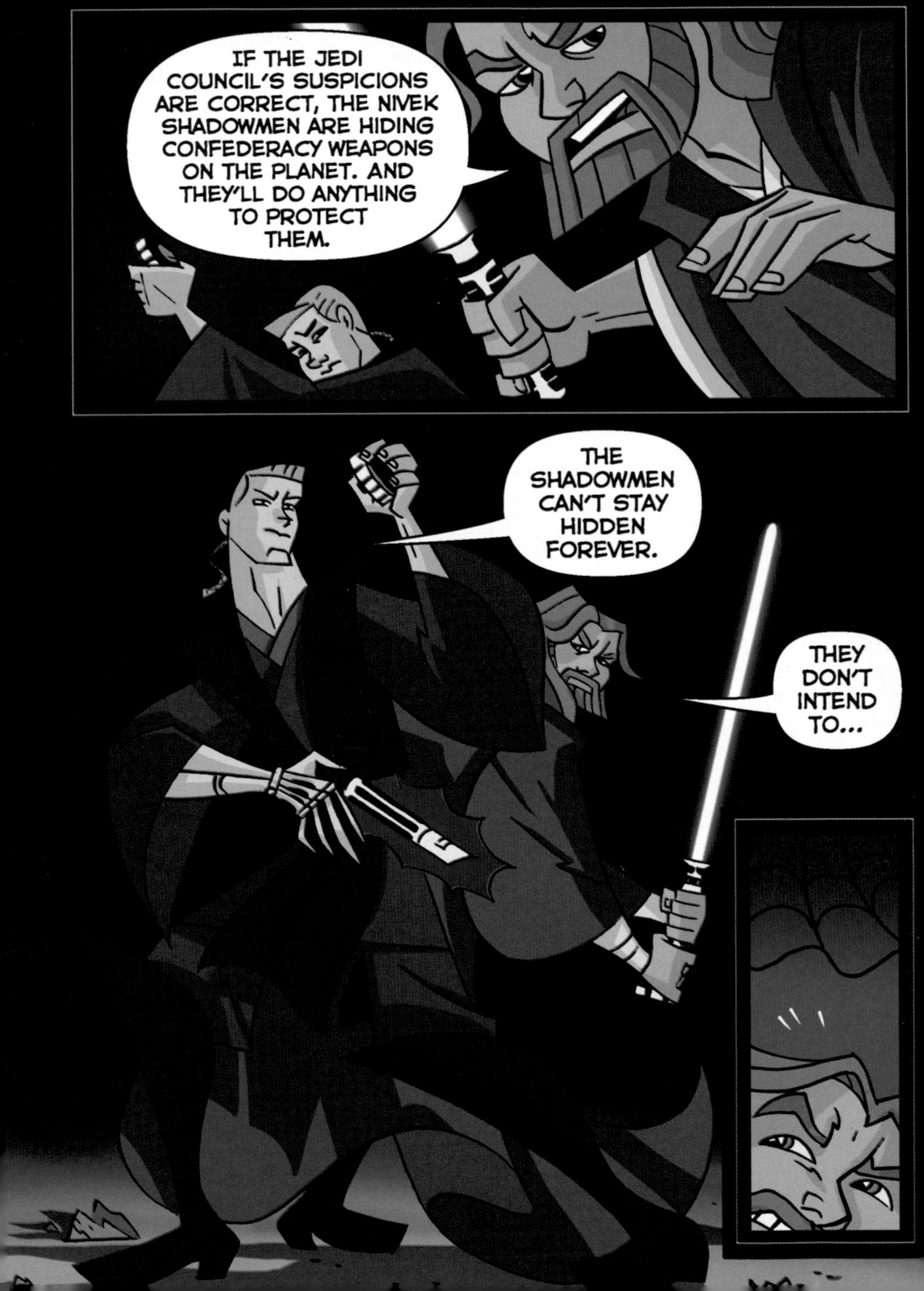
IF THE JEDI COUNCIL'S SUSPICIONS ARE CORRECT, THE NIVEK SHADOWMEN ARE HIDING CONFEDERACY WEAPONS ON THE PLANET. AND THEY'LL DO ANYTHING TO PROTECT THEM.
THE SHADOWMEN CAN'T STAY HIDDEN FOREVER.
THEY DON'T INTEND TO...

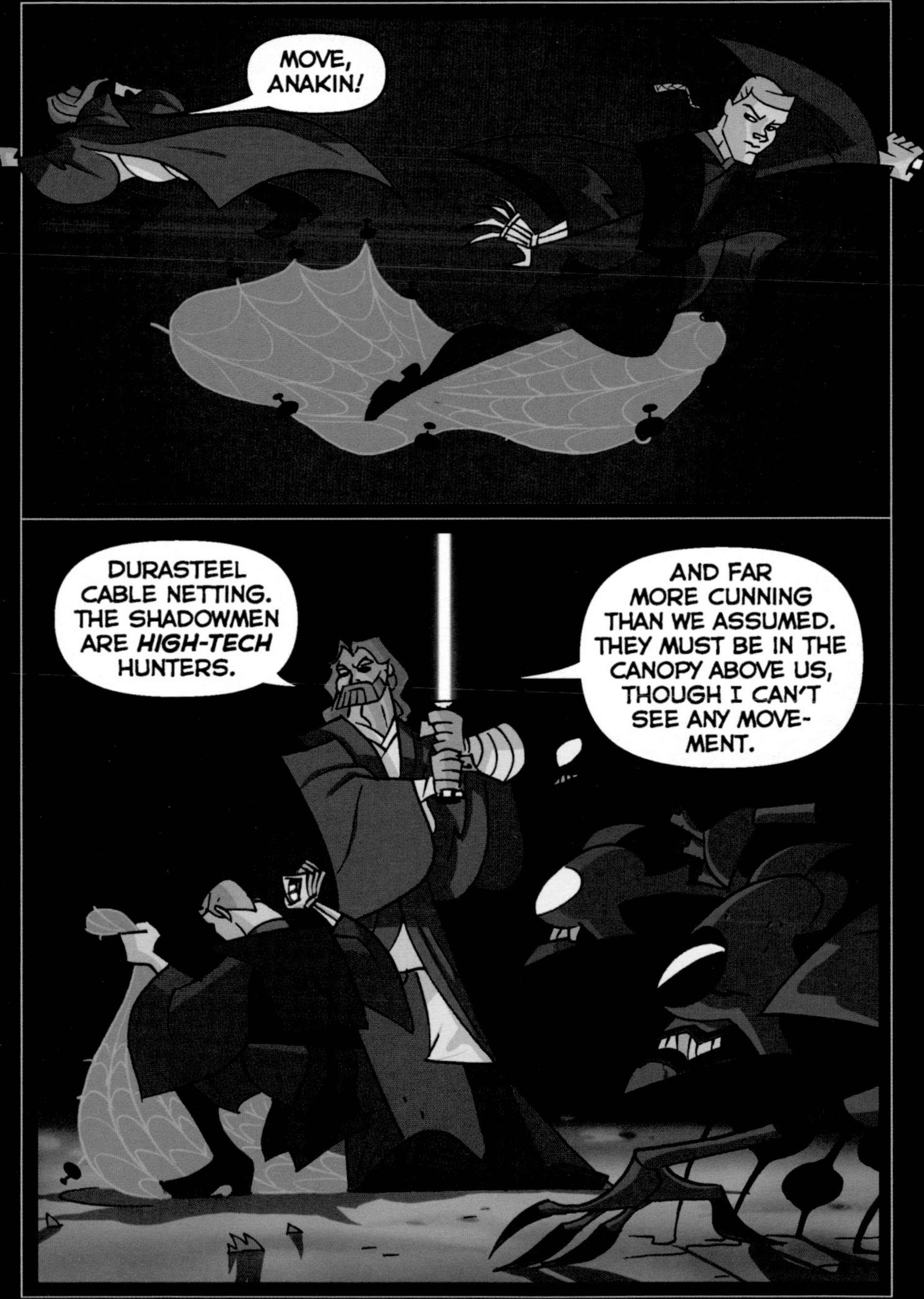
MOVE, ANAKIN!
DURASTEEL CABLE NETTING. THE SHADOWMEN ARE *HIGH-TECH* HUNTERS.
AND FAR MORE CUNNING THAN WE ASSUMED. THEY MUST BE IN THE CANOPY ABOVE US, THOUGH I CAN'T SEE ANY MOVE-MENT.

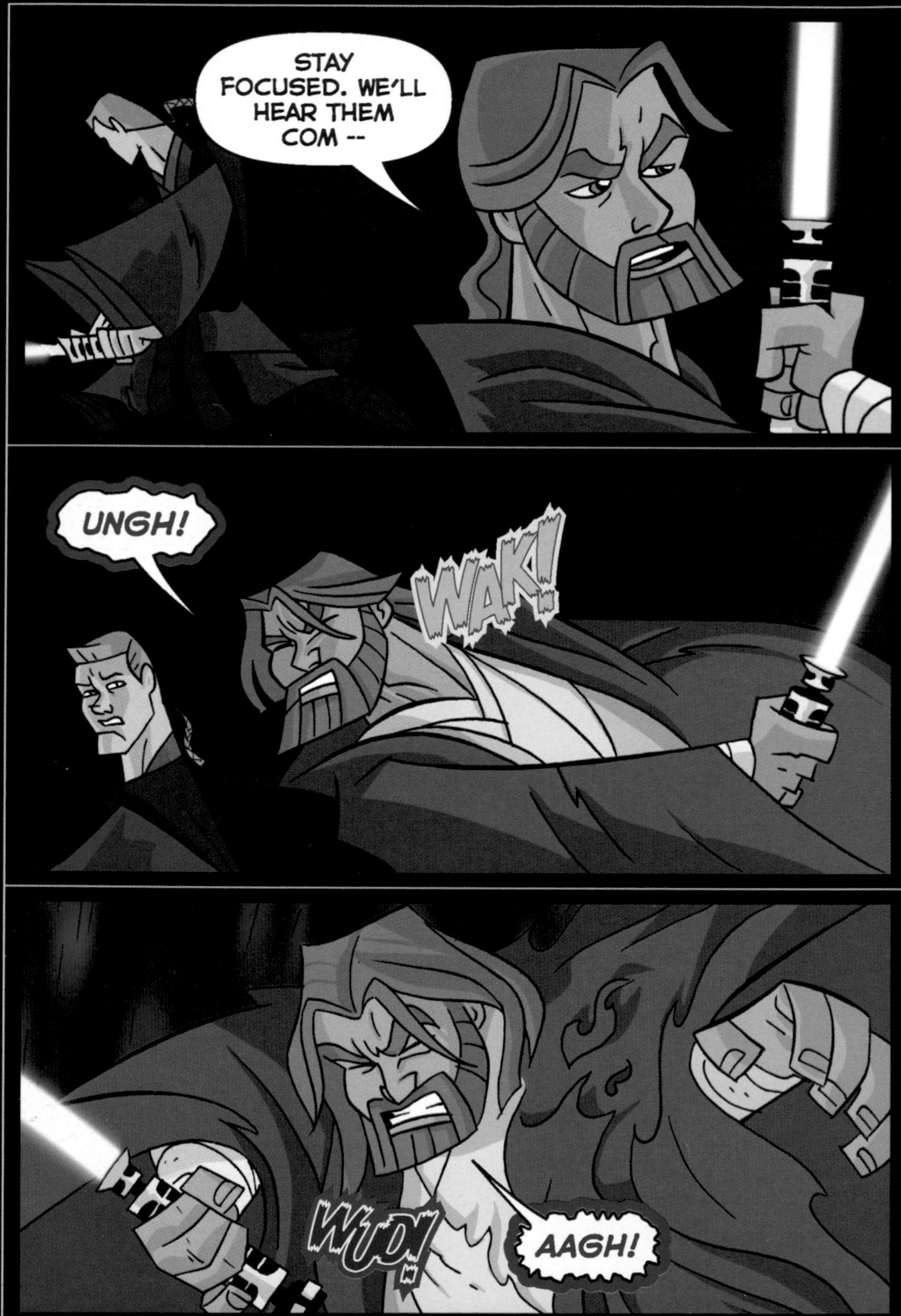
STAY FOCUSED. WE'LL HEAR THEM COM --
UNGH!
WAK!
WUD!
AAGH!

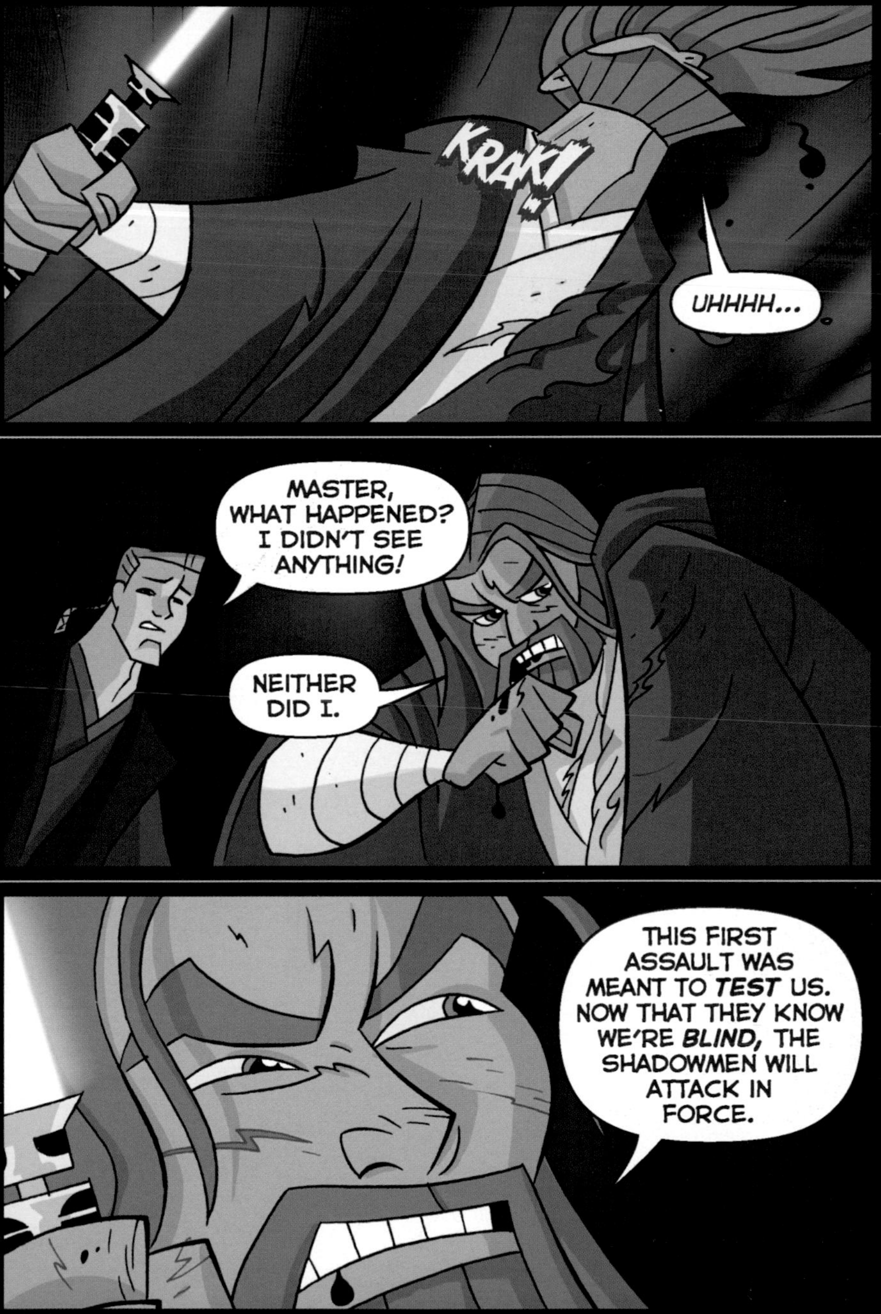
KRAK!
UHHHH...
MASTER, WHAT HAPPENED? I DIDN'T SEE ANYTHING!
NEITHER DID I.
THIS FIRST ASSAULT WAS MEANT TO TEST US. NOW THAT THEY KNOW WE'RE BLIND, THE SHADOWMEN WILL ATTACK IN FORCE.

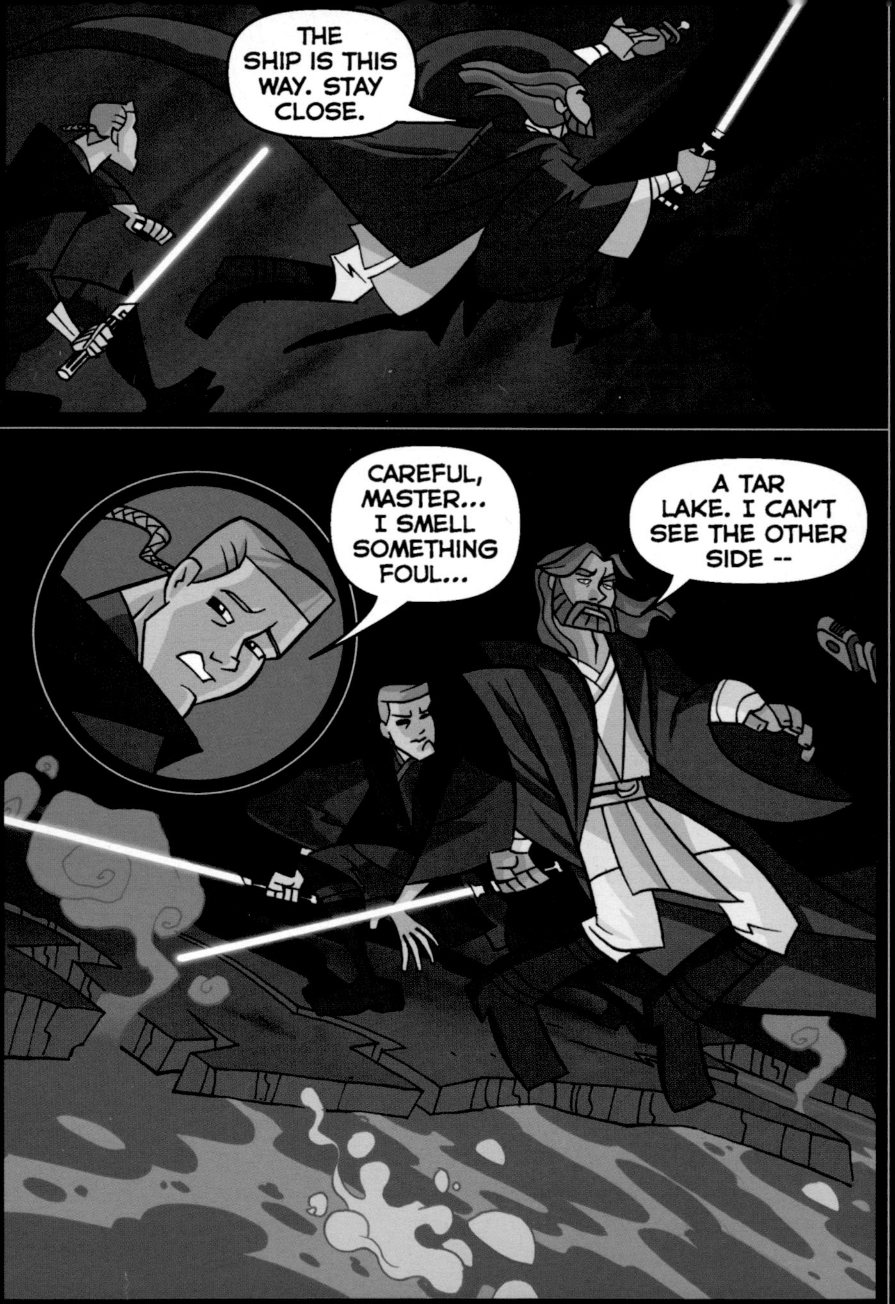
THE SHIP IS THIS WAY. STAY CLOSE.
CAREFUL, MASTER... I SMELL SOMETHING FOUL...
A TAR LAKE. I CAN'T SEE THE OTHER SIDE --

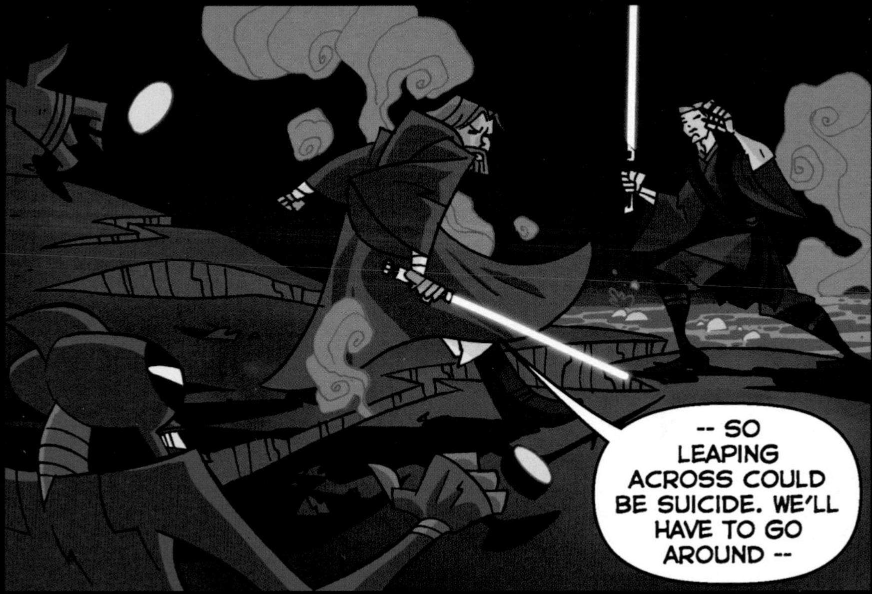
-- SO LEAPING ACROSS COULD BE SUICIDE. WE'LL HAVE TO GO AROUND --

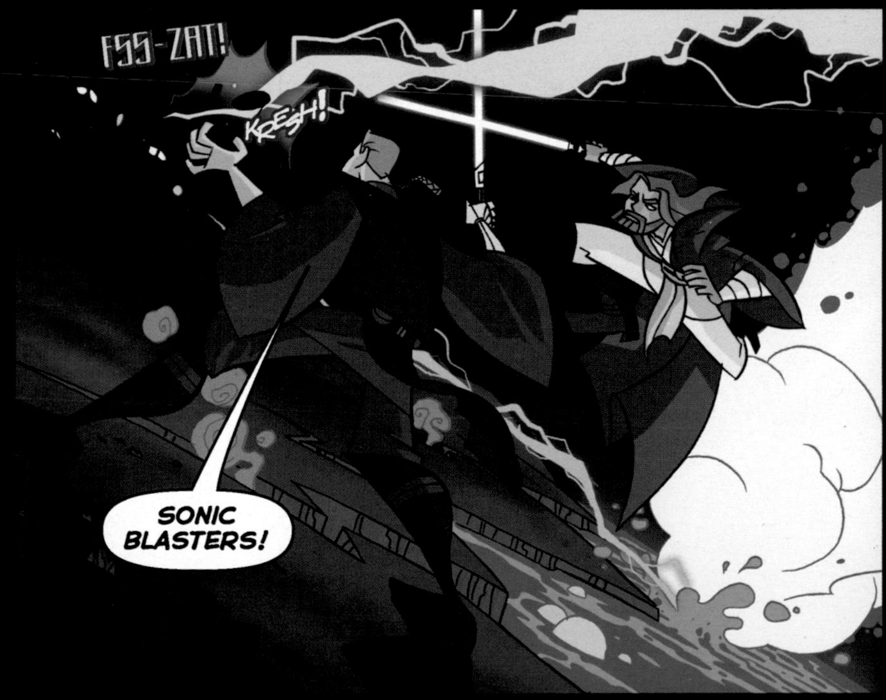
FSS-ZAT!
KRESH!
SONIC BLASTERS!

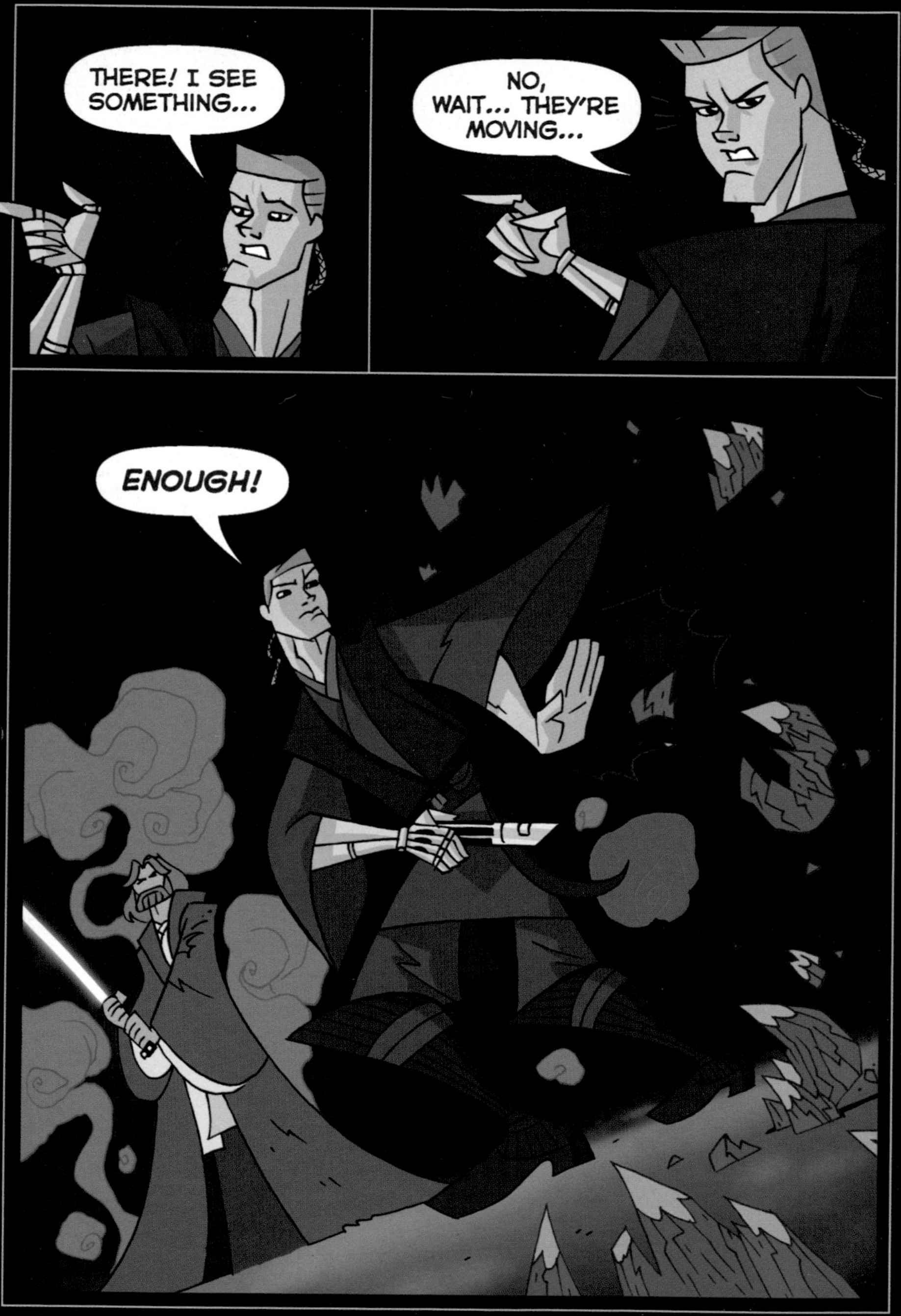
THERE! I SEE SOMETHING...
NO, WAIT... THEY'RE MOVING...
ENOUGH!

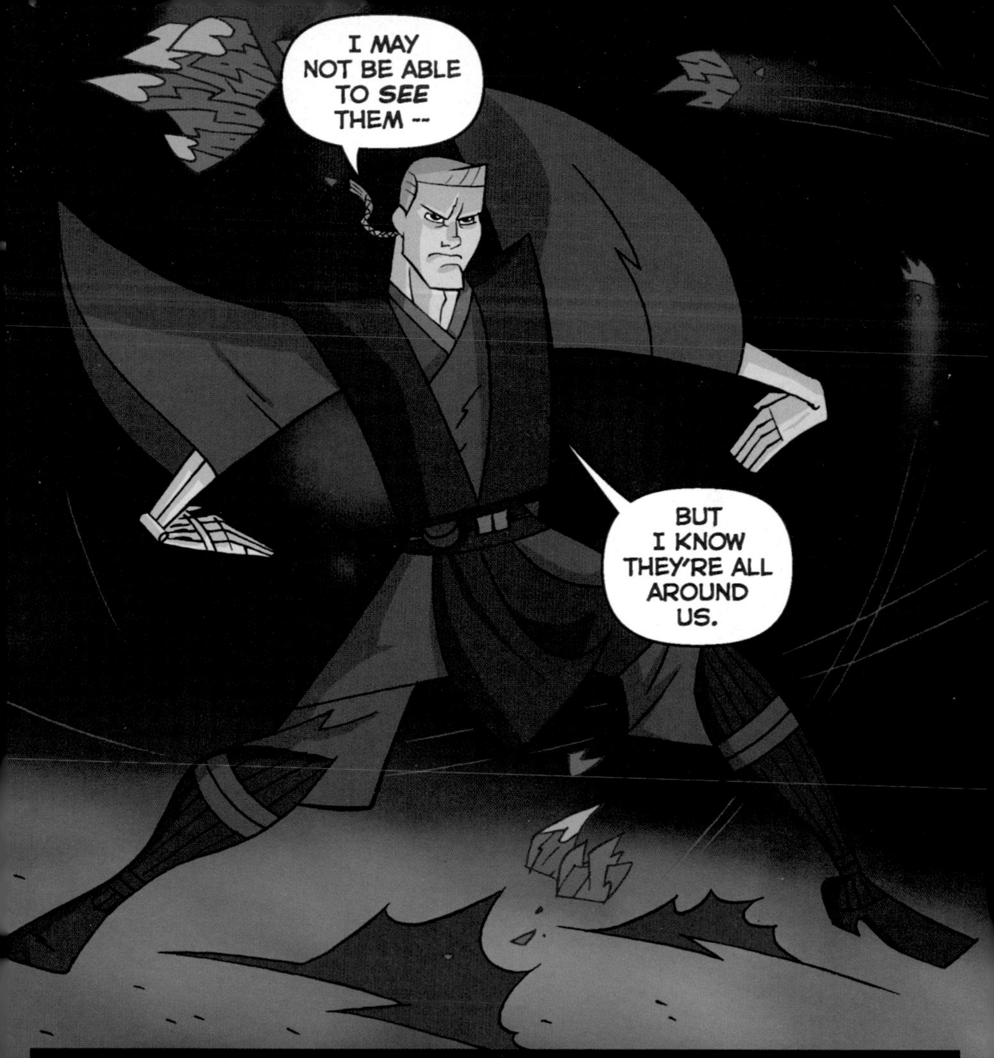
I MAY NOT BE ABLE TO *SEE* THEM --
BUT I KNOW THEY'RE ALL AROUND US.

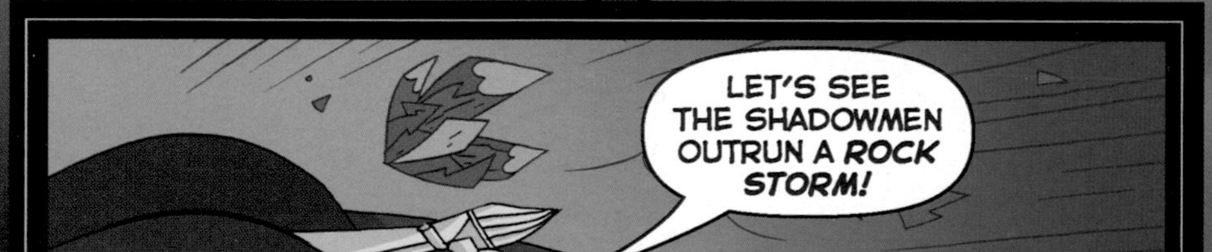
LET'S SEE THE SHADOWMEN OUTRUN A *ROCK STORM!*

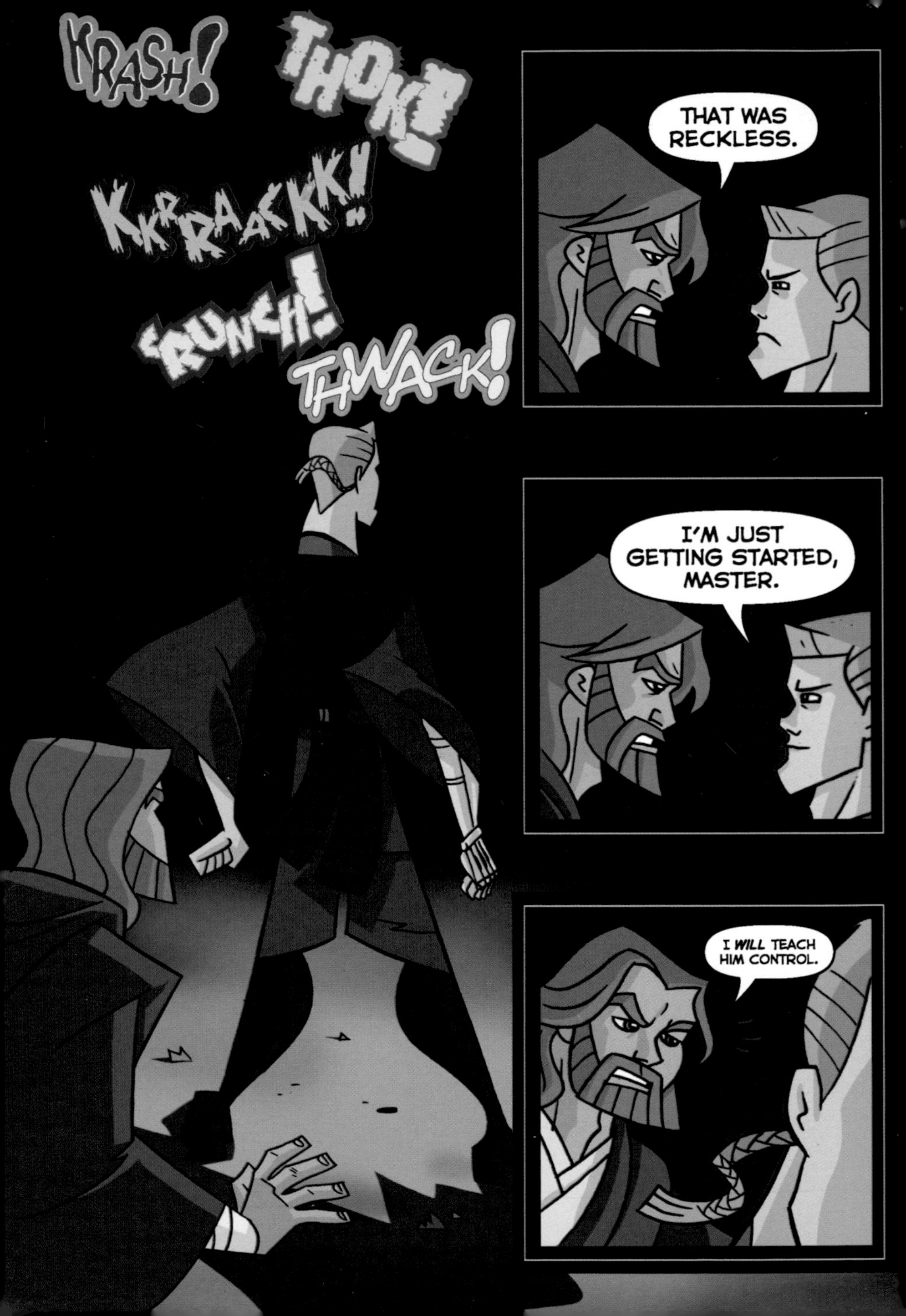
KRASH!
THOK!
KKRRAACKK!
CRUNCH!
THWACK!
THAT WAS RECKLESS.
I'M JUST GETTING STARTED, MASTER.
I WILL TEACH HIM CONTROL.

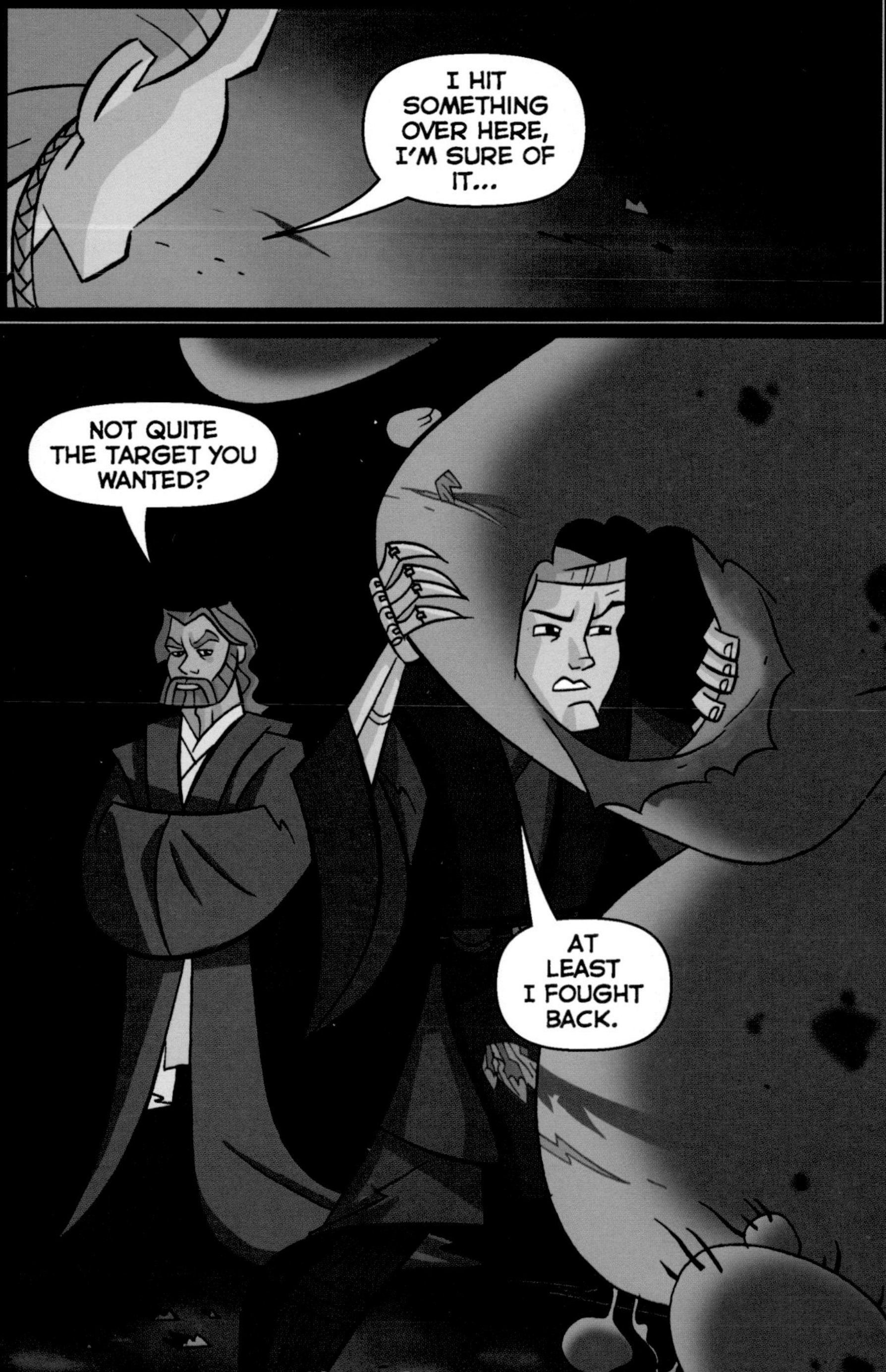
I HIT SOMETHING OVER HERE, I'M SURE OF IT...
NOT QUITE THE TARGET YOU WANTED?
AT LEAST I FOUGHT BACK.

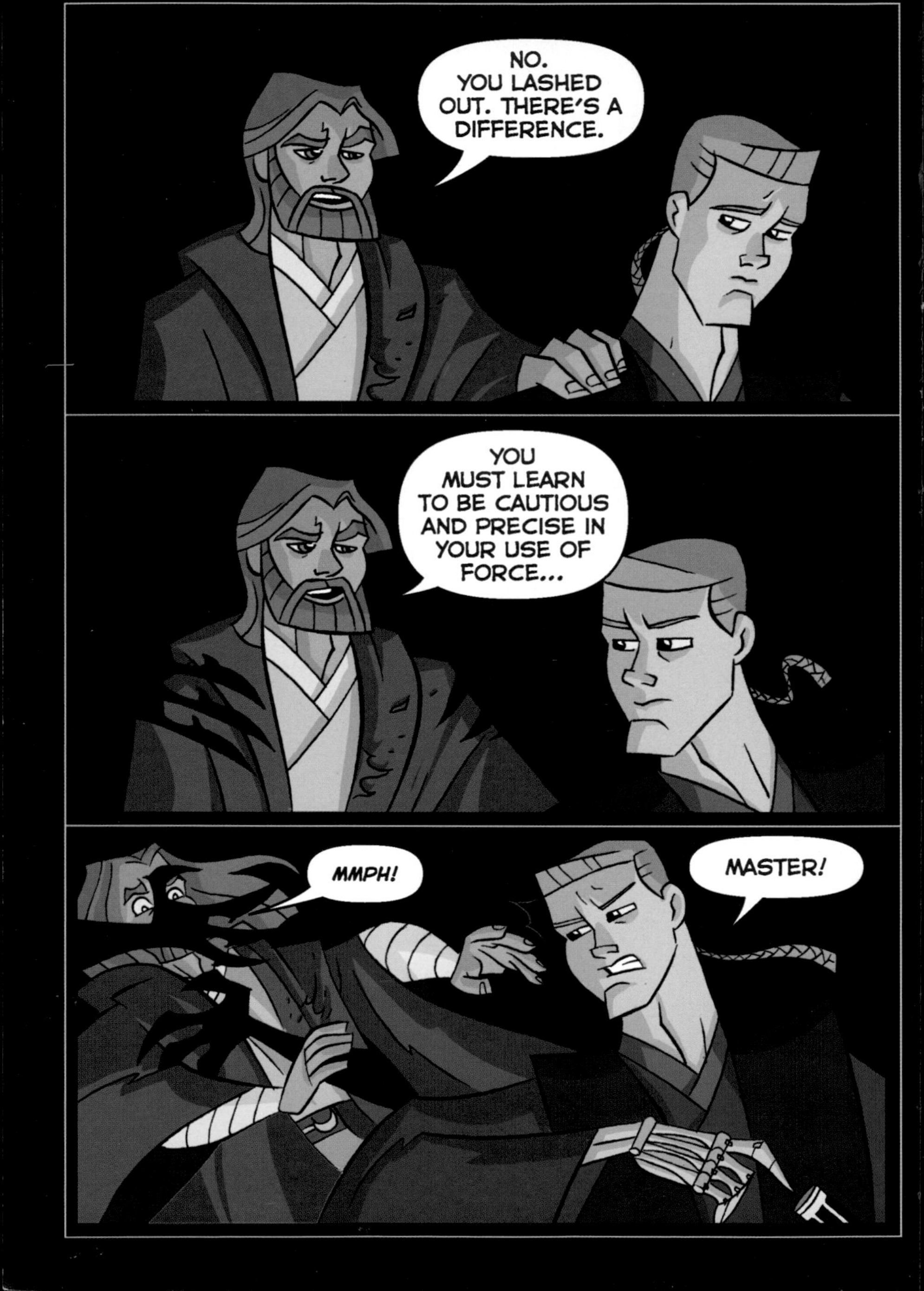
NO. YOU LASHED OUT. THERE'S A DIFFERENCE.
YOU MUST LEARN TO BE CAUTIOUS AND PRECISE IN YOUR USE OF FORCE...
MMPH!
MASTER!

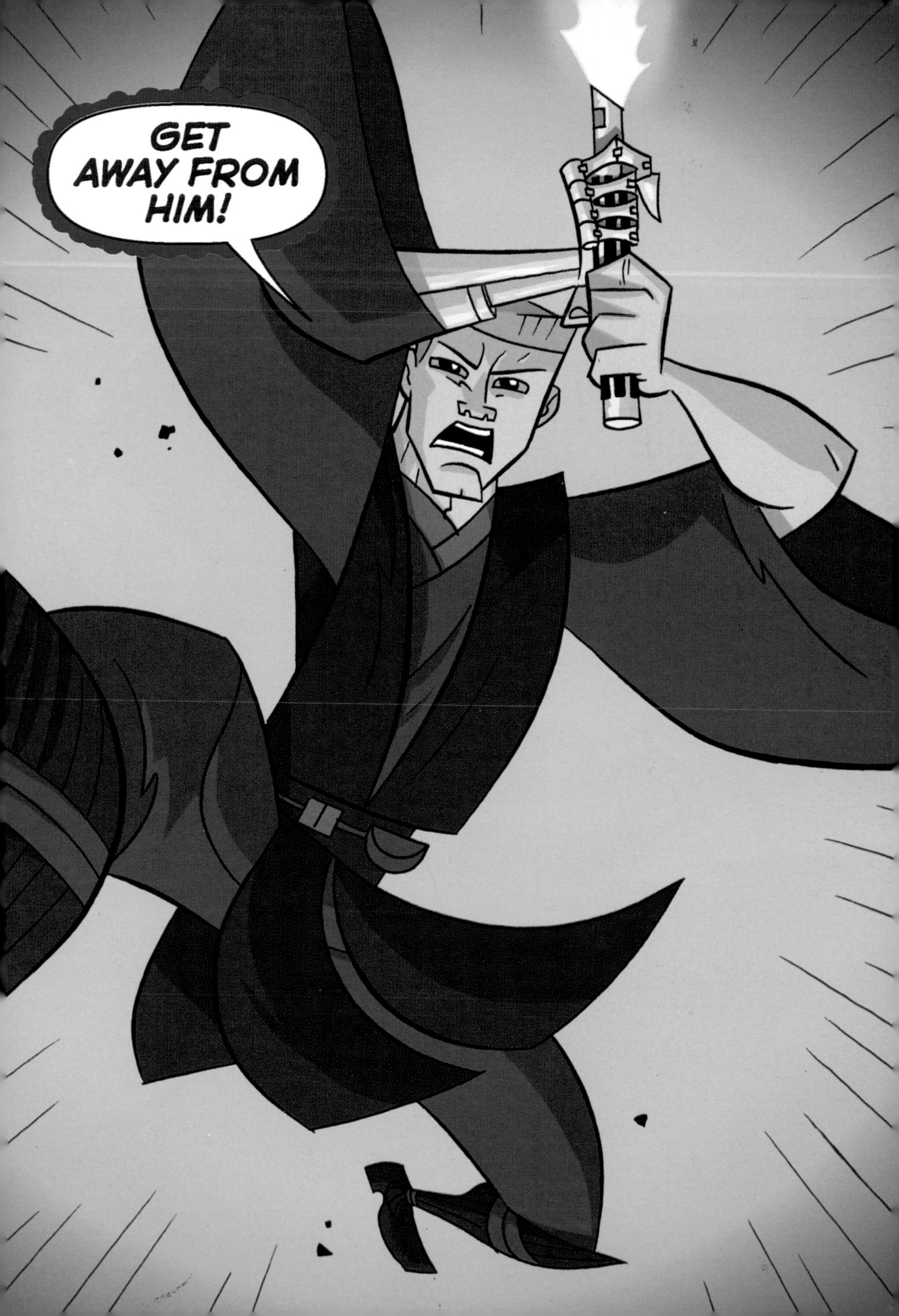
GET AWAY FROM HIM!

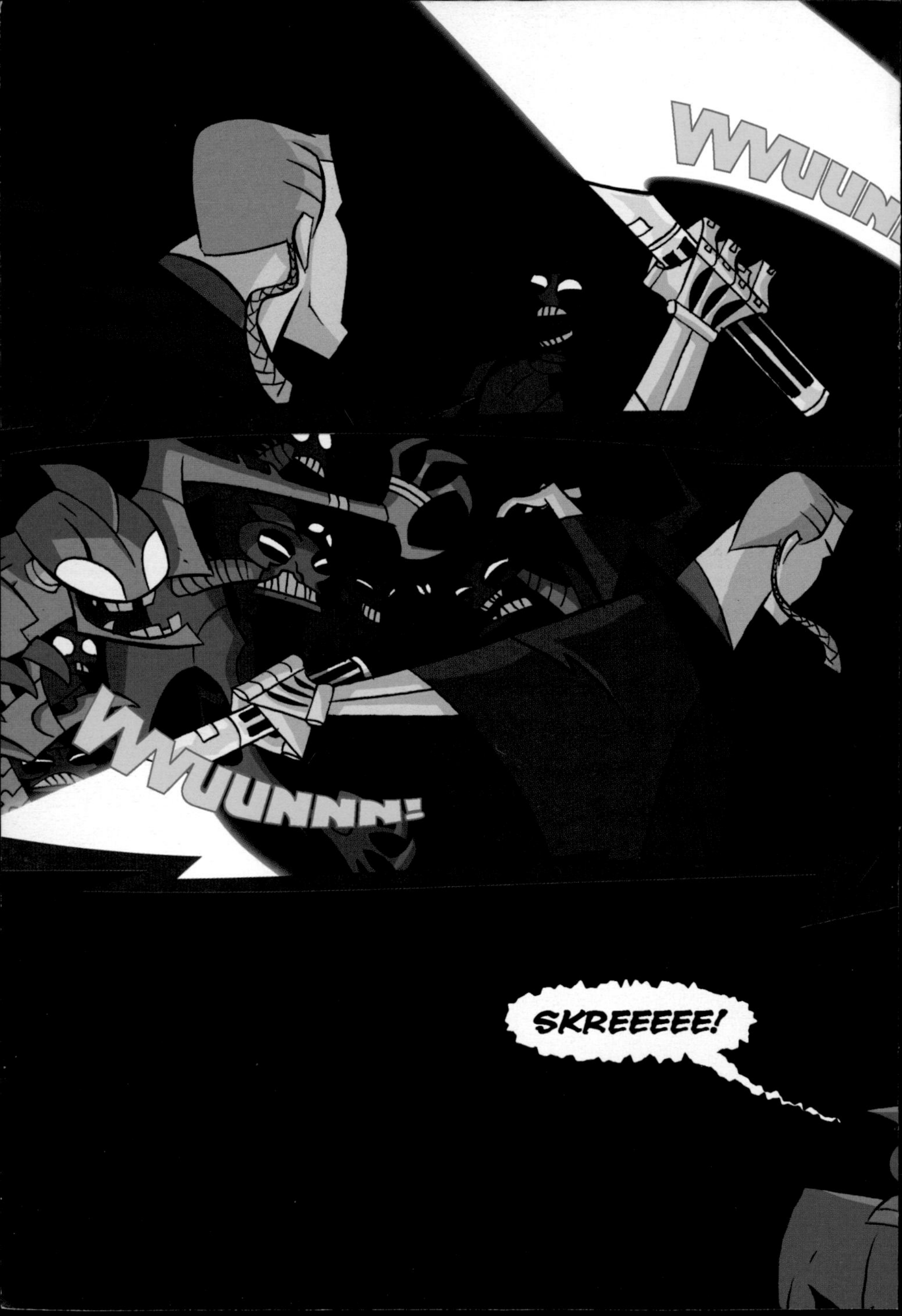
WWUUNN
WWUUNNNN!
SKREEEEEE!

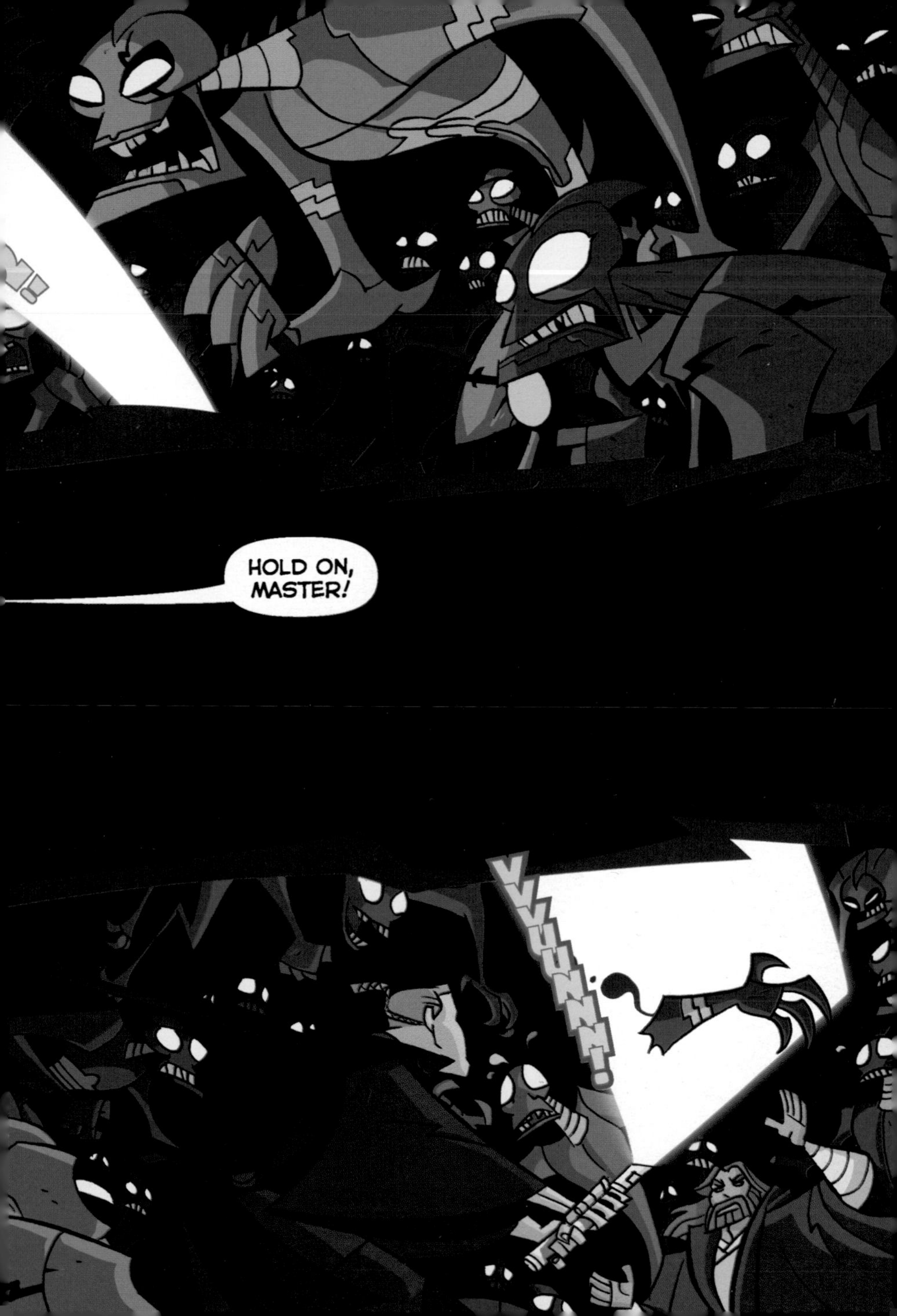
HOLD ON, MASTER!
VVUUNNN!

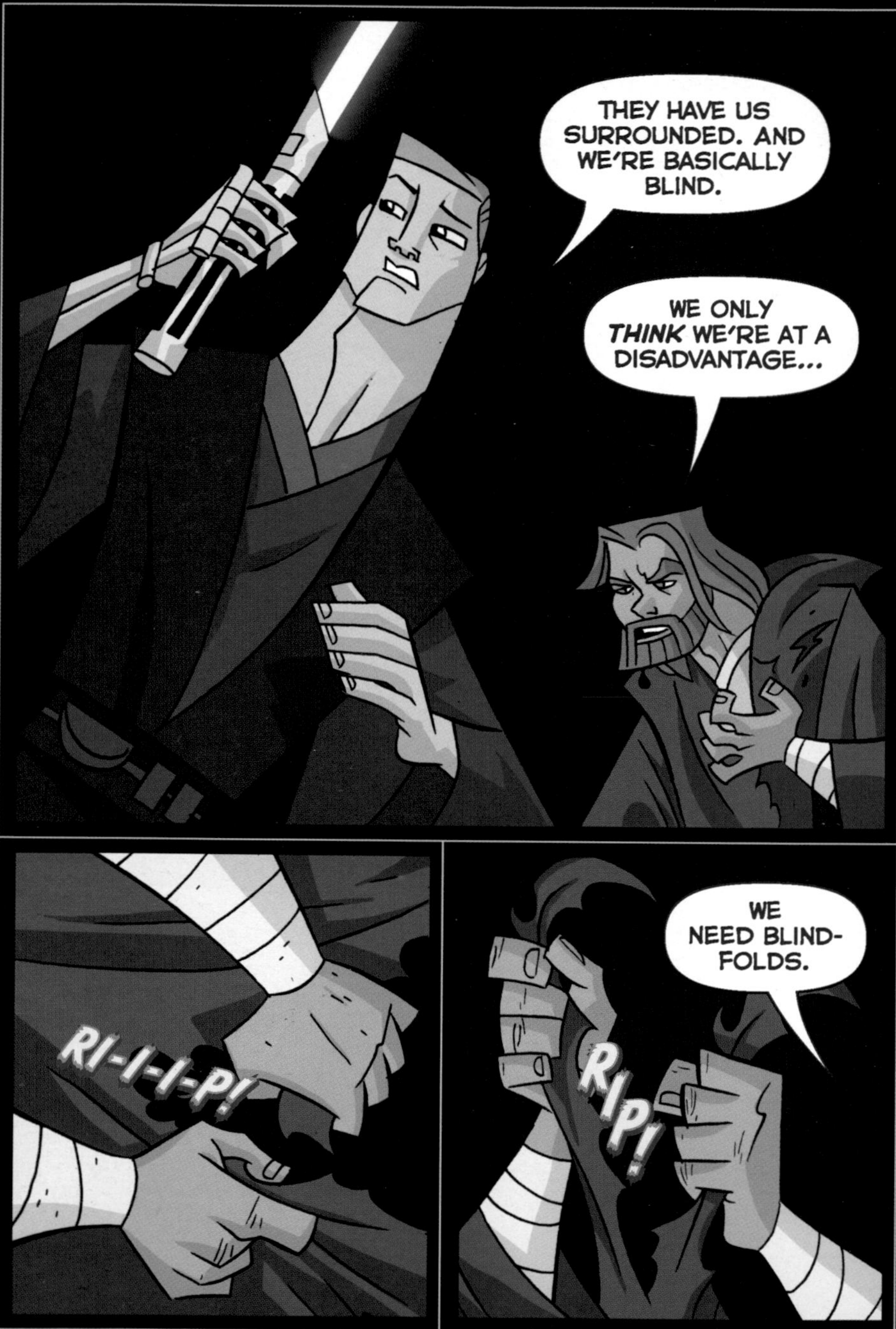
THEY HAVE US SURROUNDED. AND WE'RE BASICALLY BLIND.
WE ONLY *THINK* WE'RE AT A DISADVANTAGE...
RI-I-I-P!
RIP!
WE NEED BLIND-FOLDS.

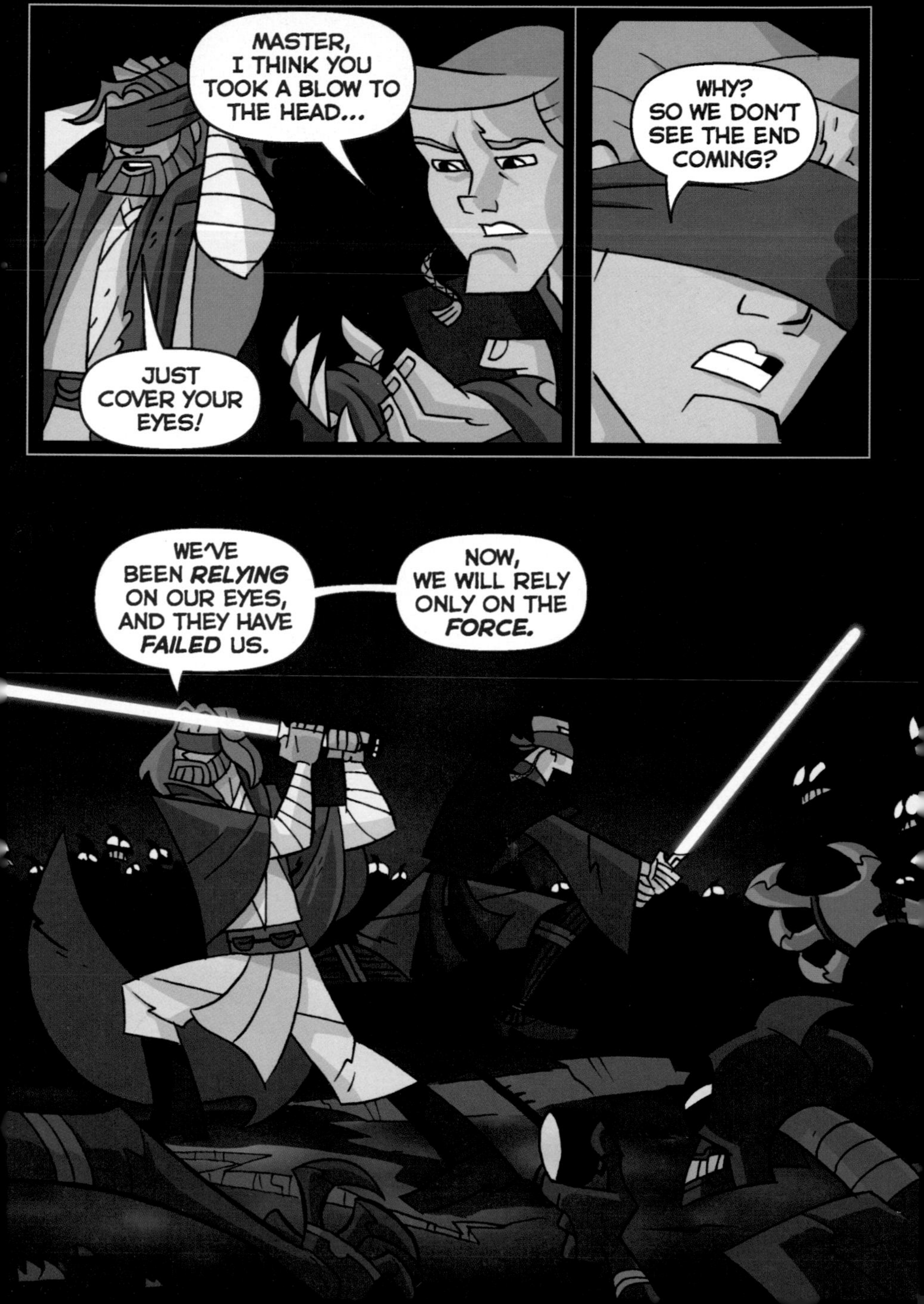
MASTER, I THINK YOU TOOK A BLOW TO THE HEAD...
JUST COVER YOUR EYES!
WHY? SO WE DON'T SEE THE END COMING?
WE'VE BEEN *RELYING* ON OUR EYES, AND THEY HAVE *FAILED* US.
NOW, WE WILL RELY ONLY ON THE *FORCE.*

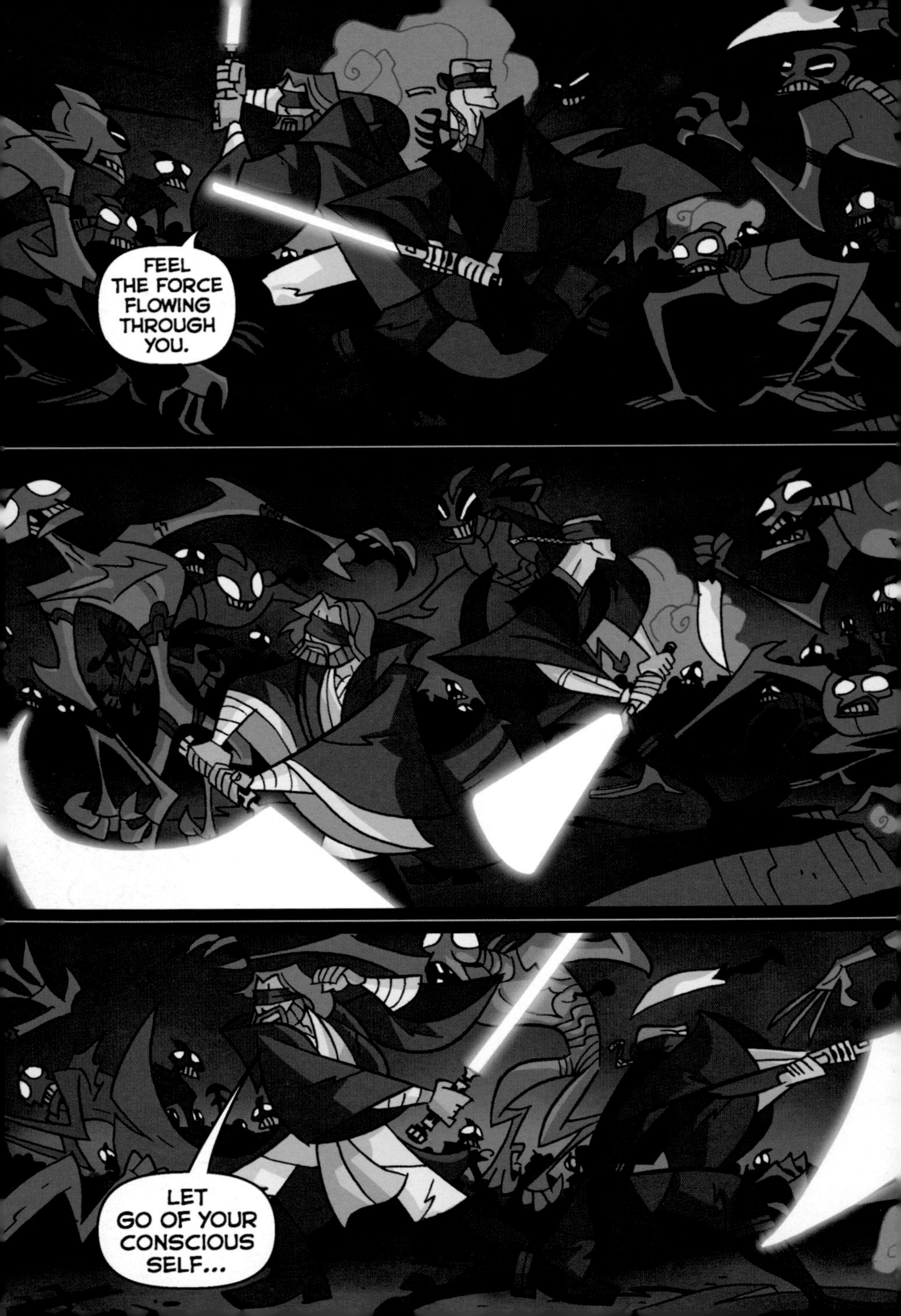
FEEL THE FORCE FLOWING THROUGH YOU.
LET GO OF YOUR CONSCIOUS SELF...

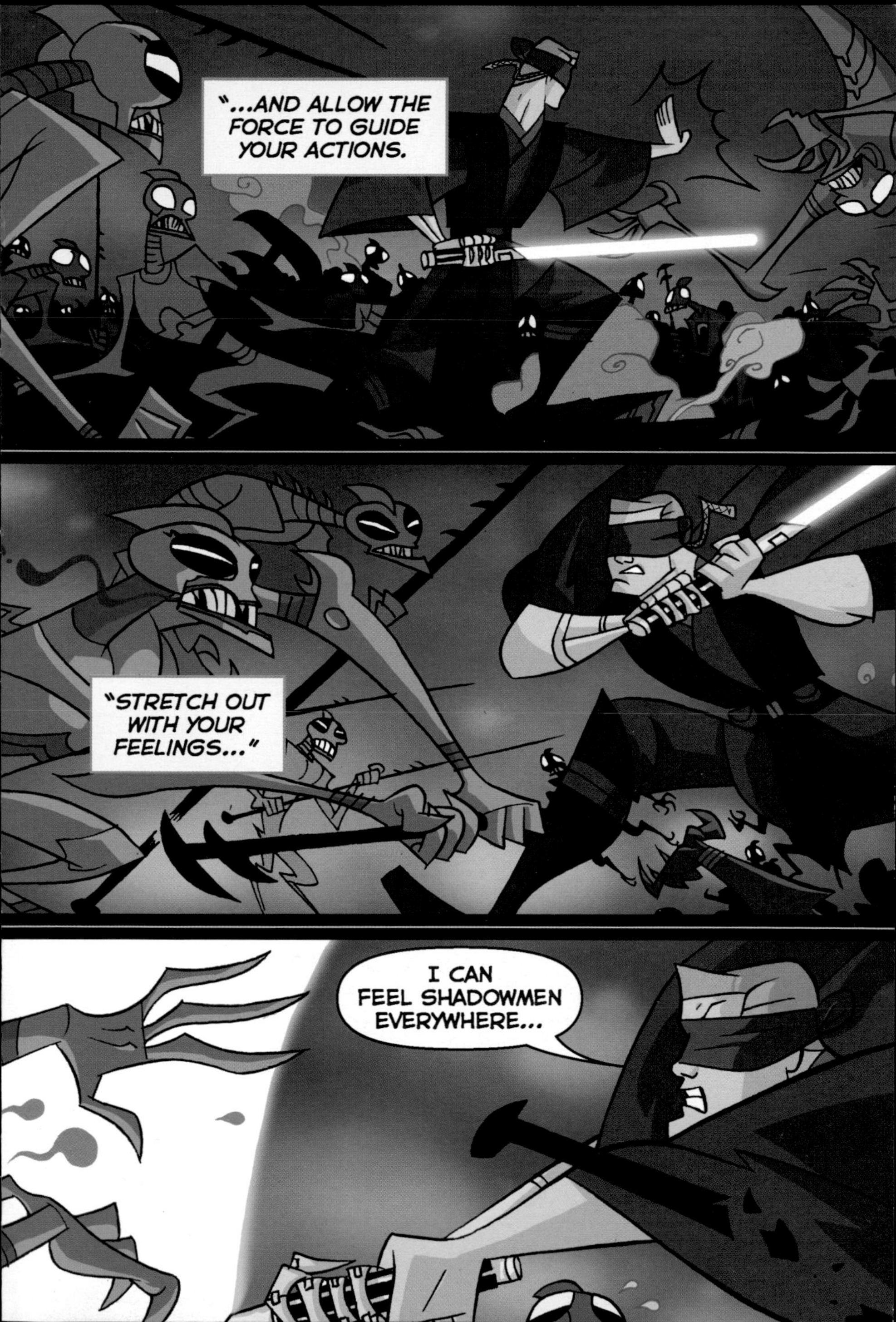
"...AND ALLOW THE FORCE TO GUIDE YOUR ACTIONS.
"STRETCH OUT WITH YOUR FEELINGS..."
I CAN FEEL SHADOWMEN EVERYWHERE...

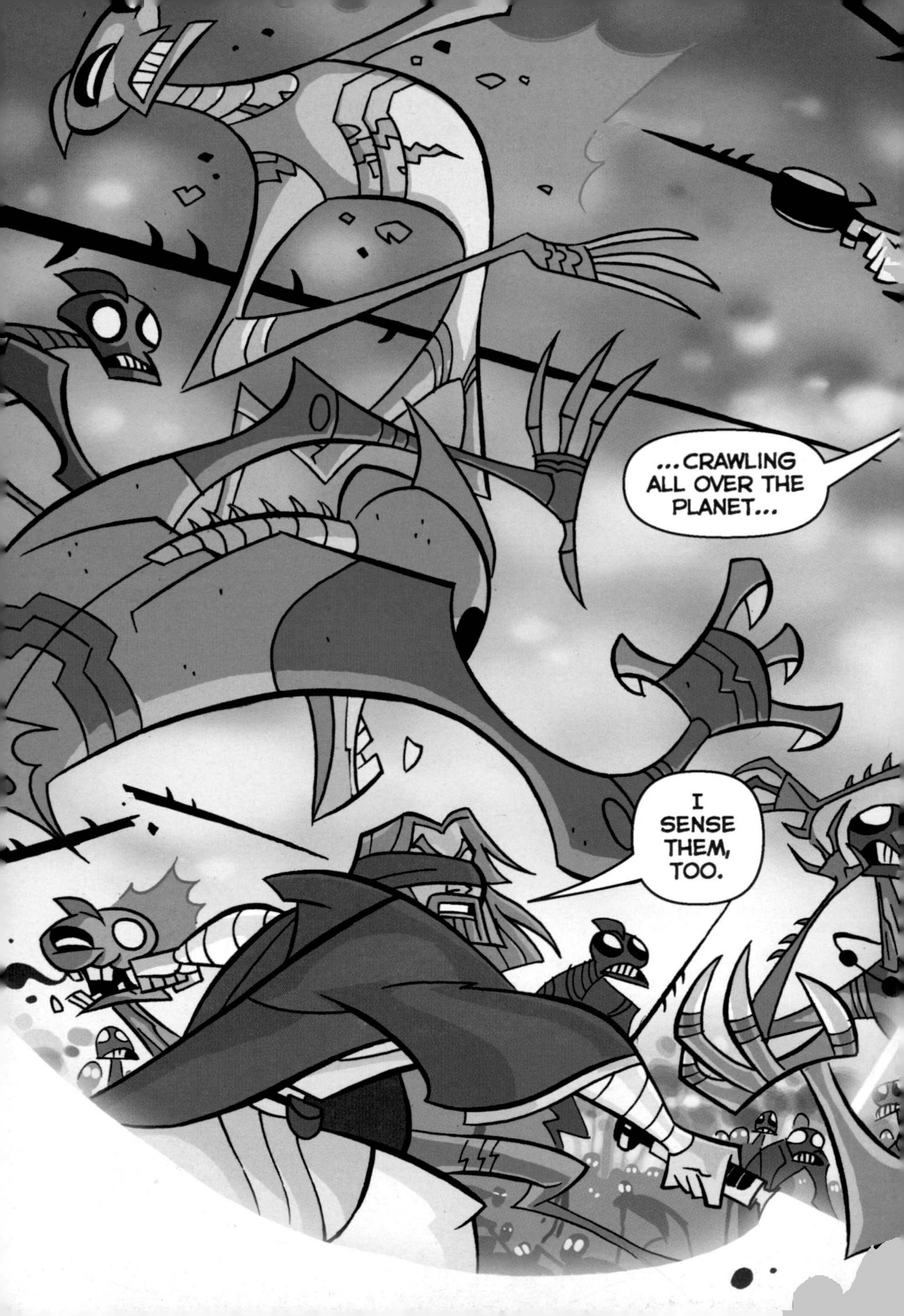
...CRAWLING ALL OVER THE PLANET...
I SENSE THEM, TOO.

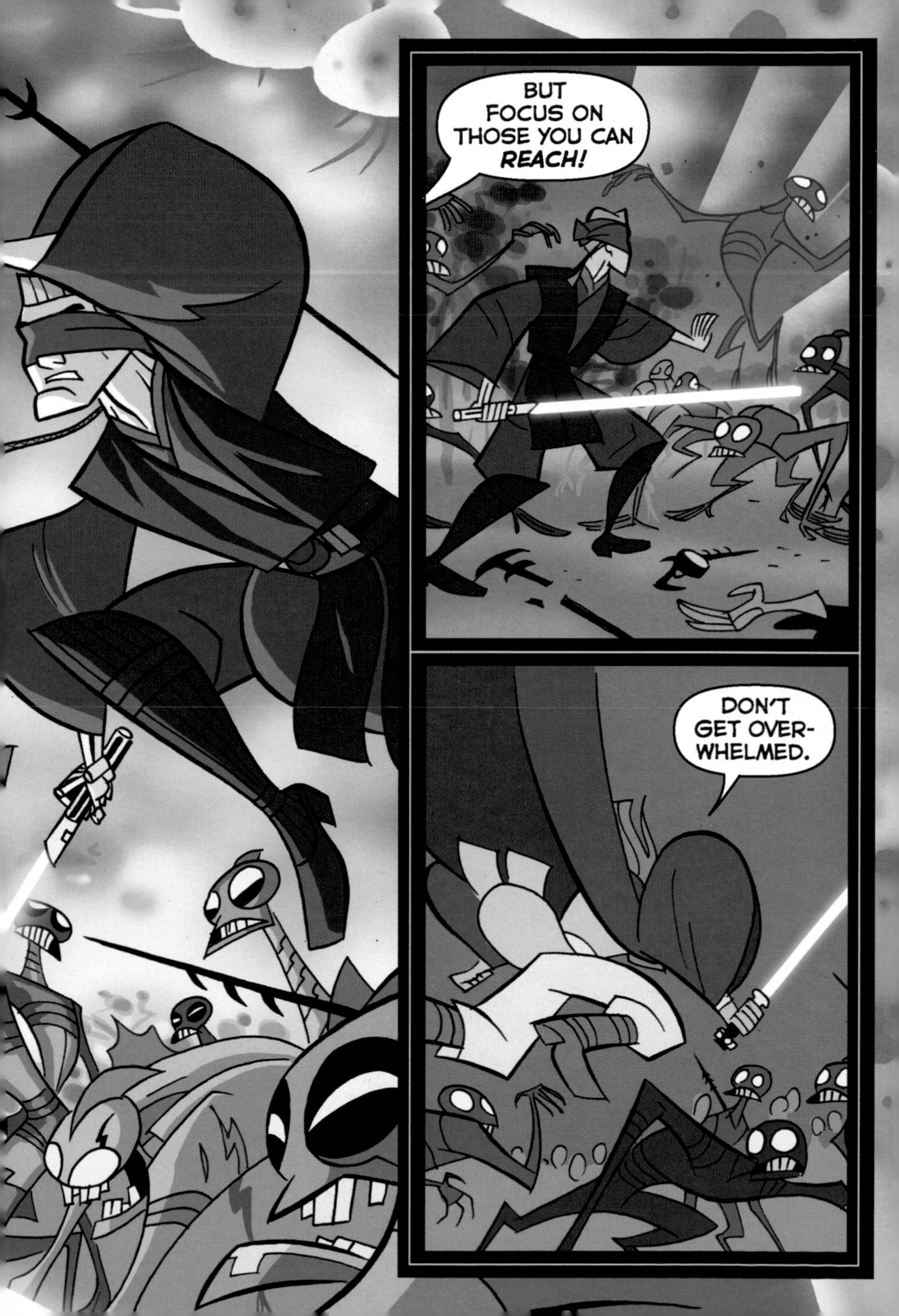
BUT FOCUS ON THOSE YOU CAN *REACH!*
DON'T GET OVER-WHELMED.

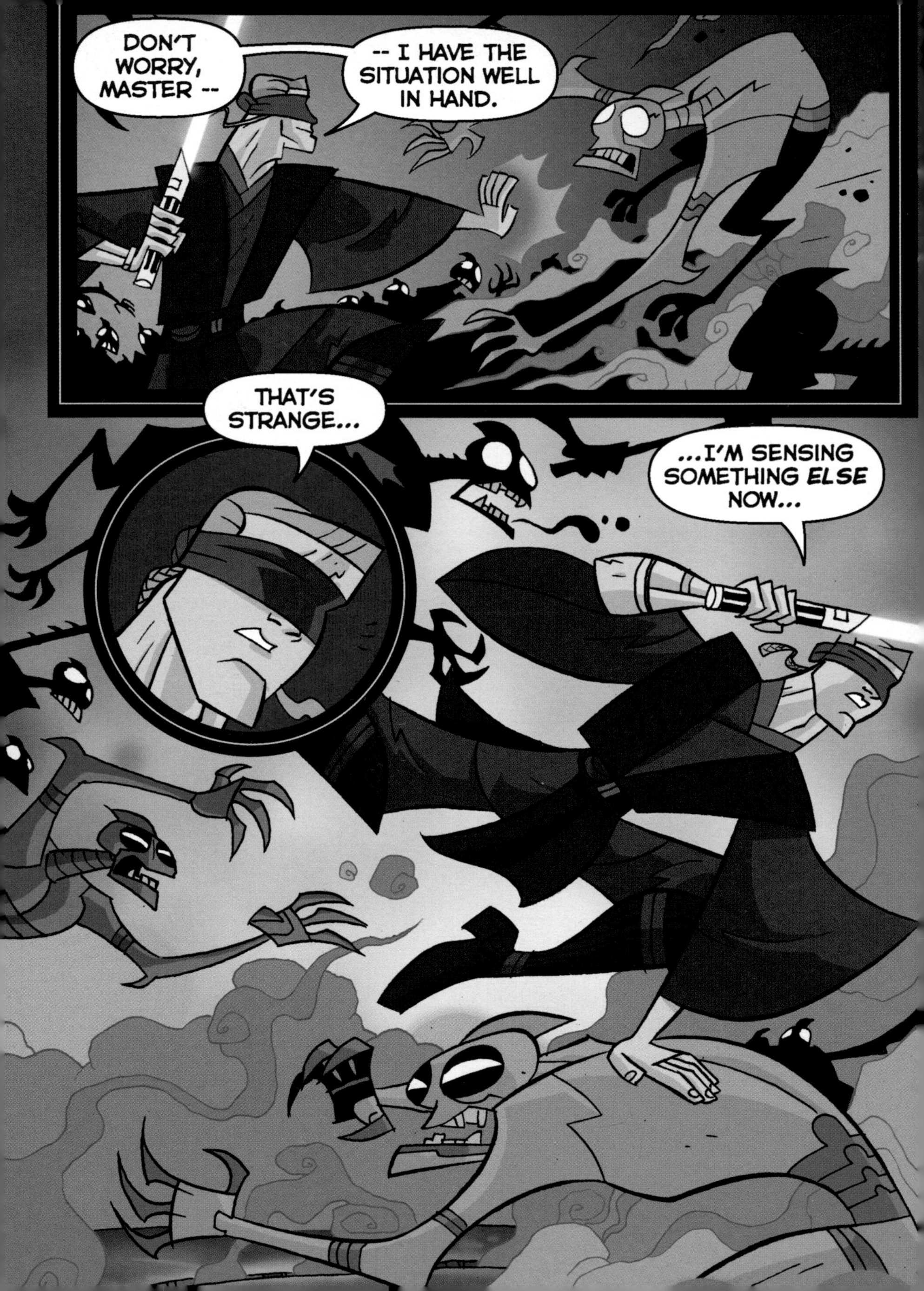
DON'T WORRY, MASTER --
-- I HAVE THE SITUATION WELL IN HAND.
THAT'S STRANGE...
...I'M SENSING SOMETHING ELSE NOW...

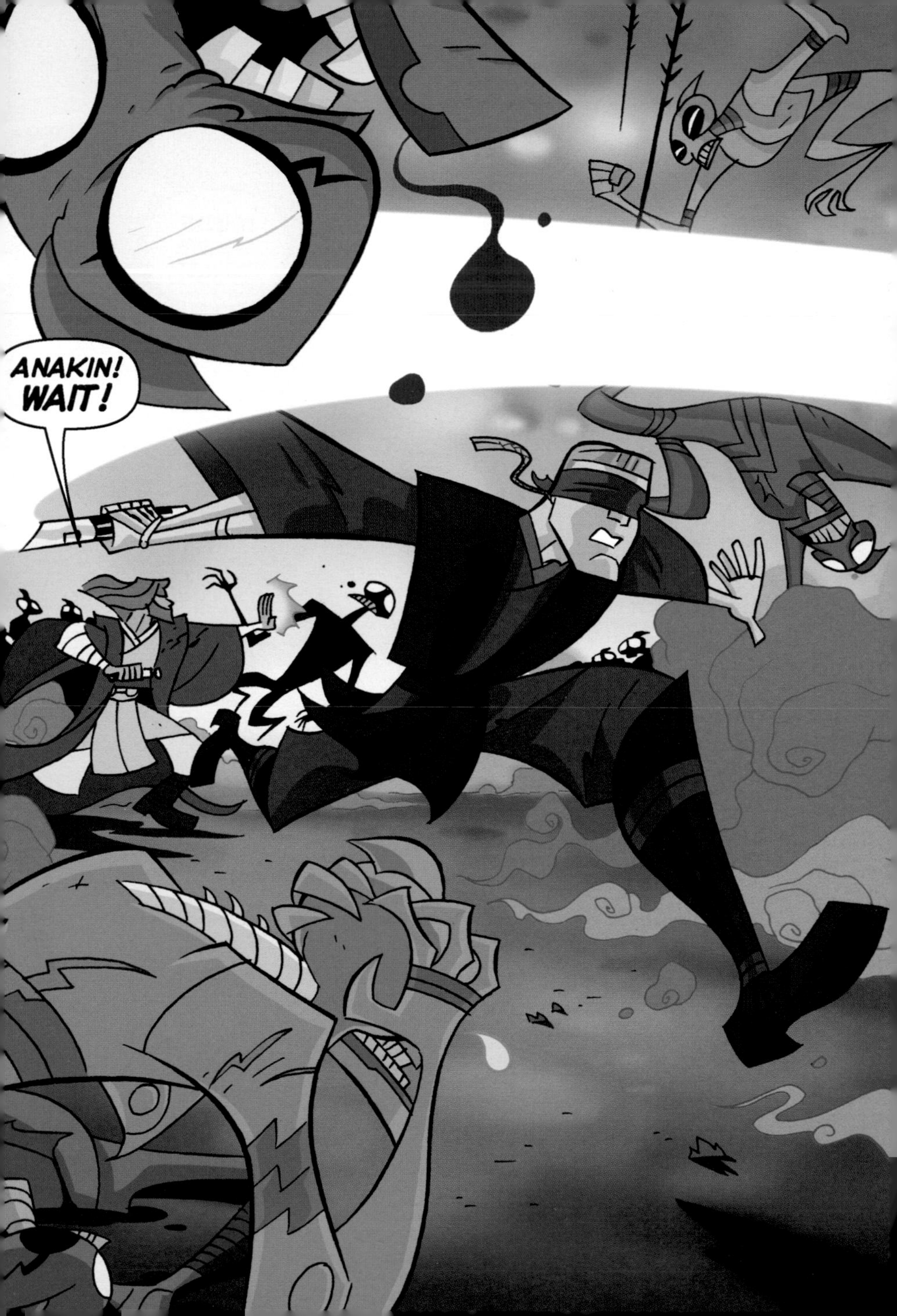
ANAKIN! WAIT!

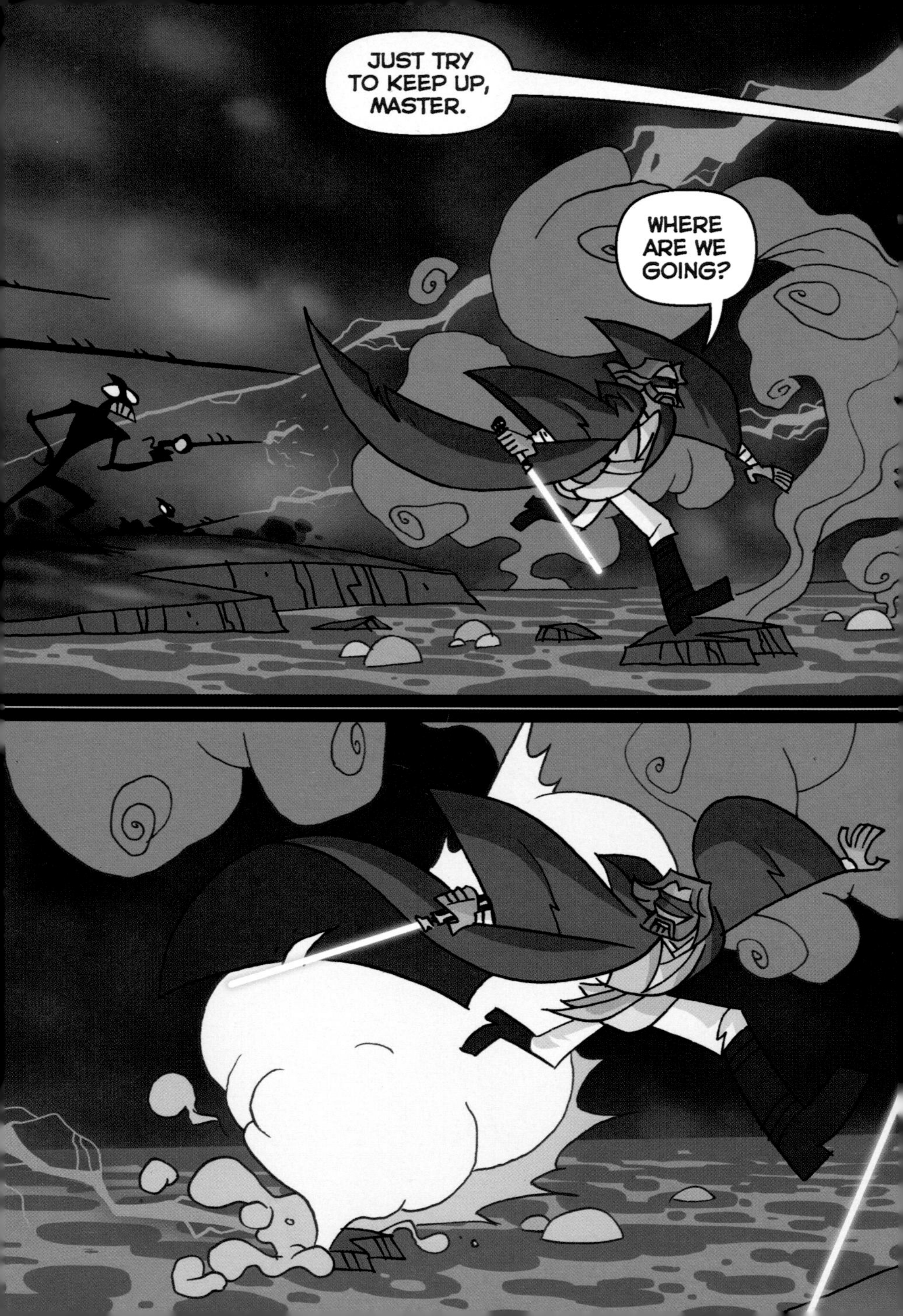
JUST TRY TO KEEP UP, MASTER.
WHERE ARE WE GOING?

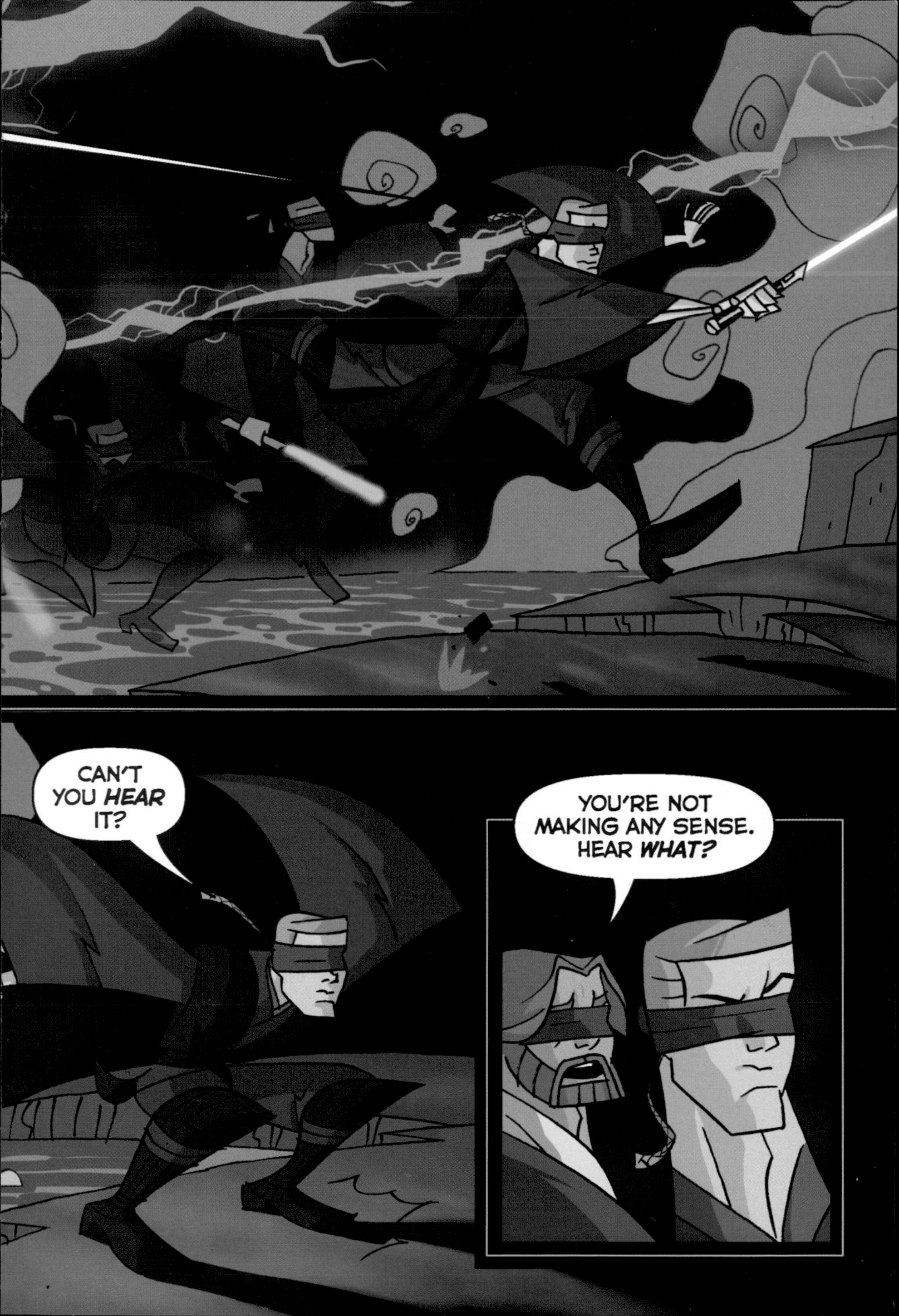
CAN'T YOU *HEAR* IT?
YOU'RE NOT MAKING ANY SENSE. HEAR *WHAT?*

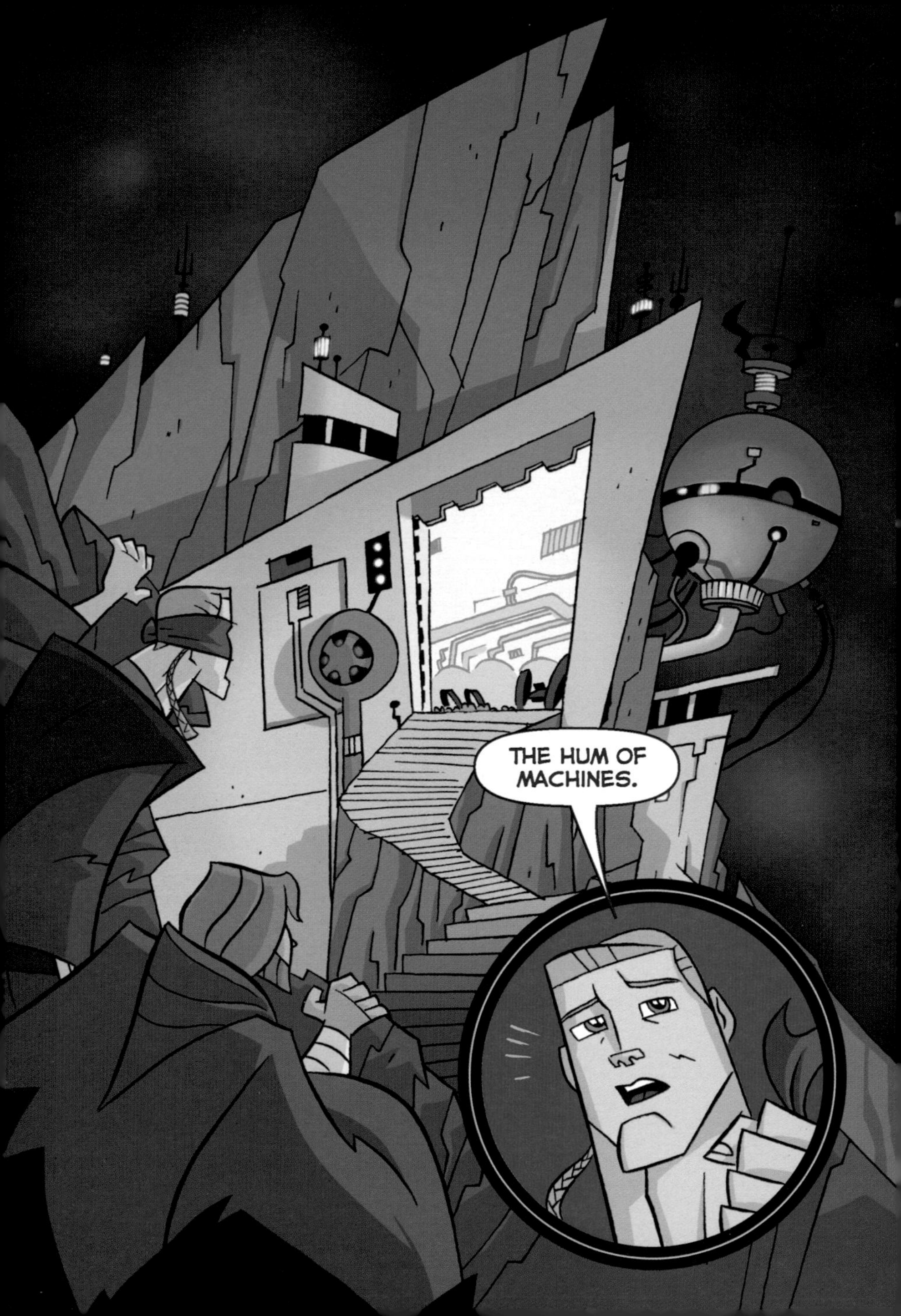
THE HUM OF MACHINES.

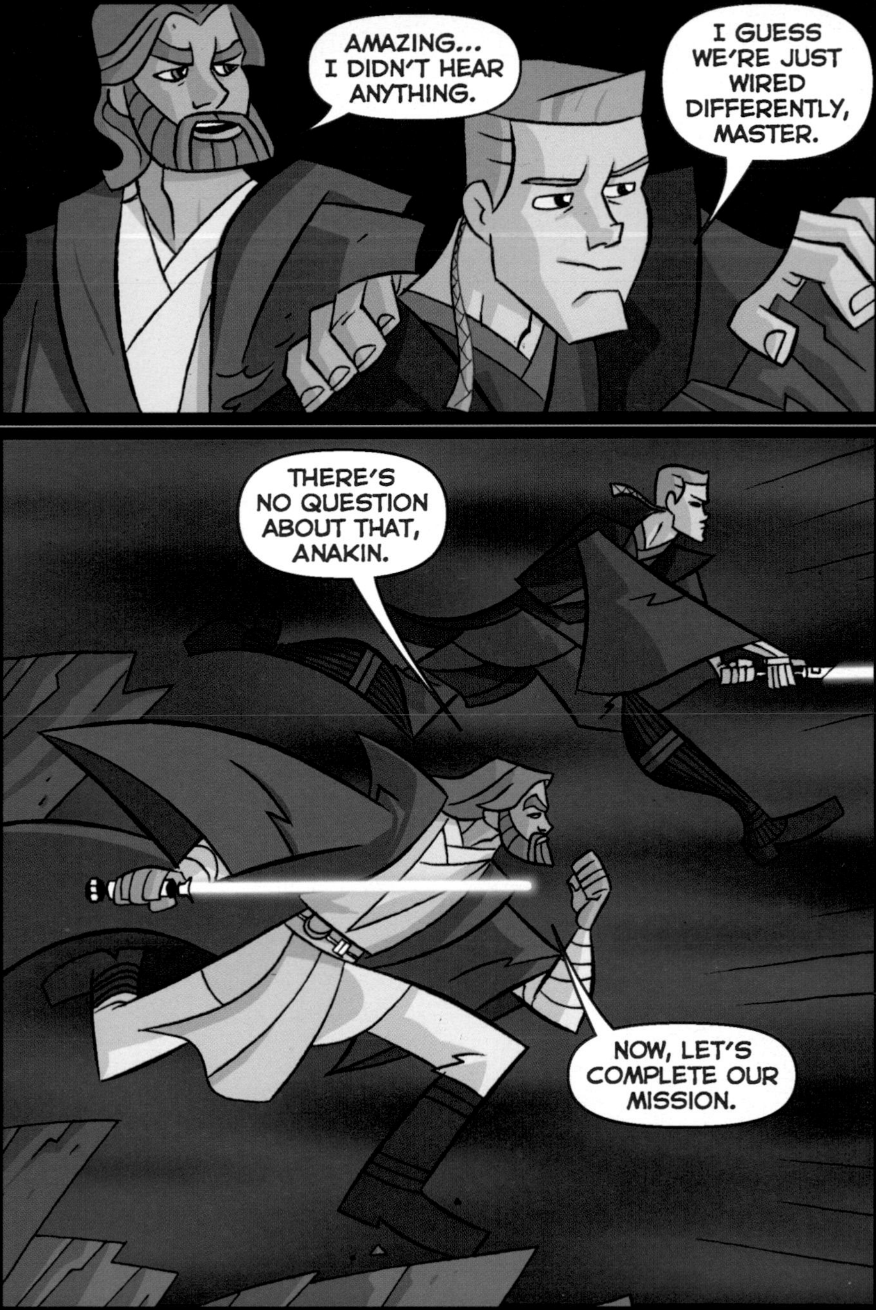
AMAZING... I DIDN'T HEAR ANYTHING.
I GUESS WE'RE JUST WIRED DIFFERENTLY, MASTER.
THERE'S NO QUESTION ABOUT THAT, ANAKIN.
NOW, LET'S COMPLETE OUR MISSION.

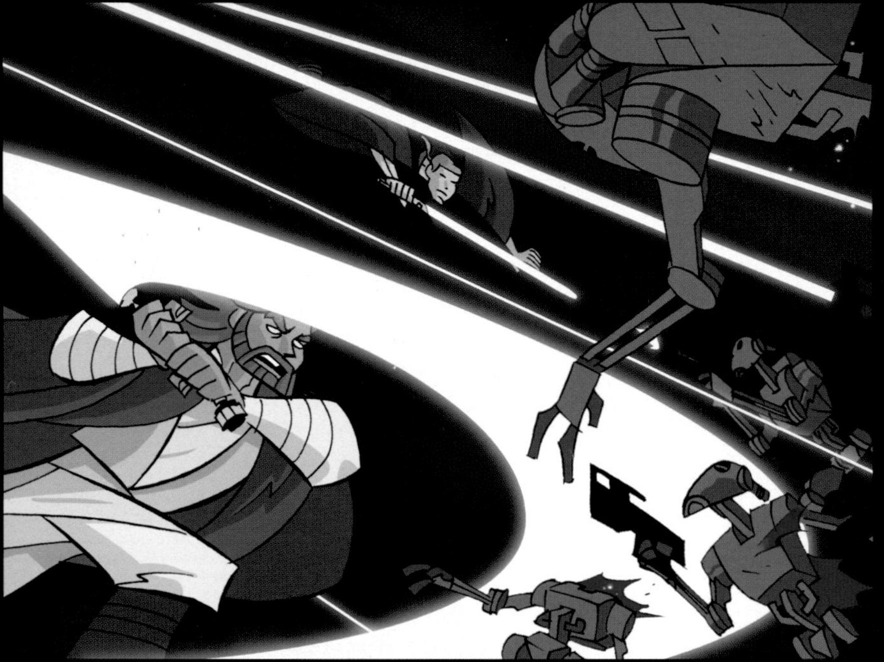

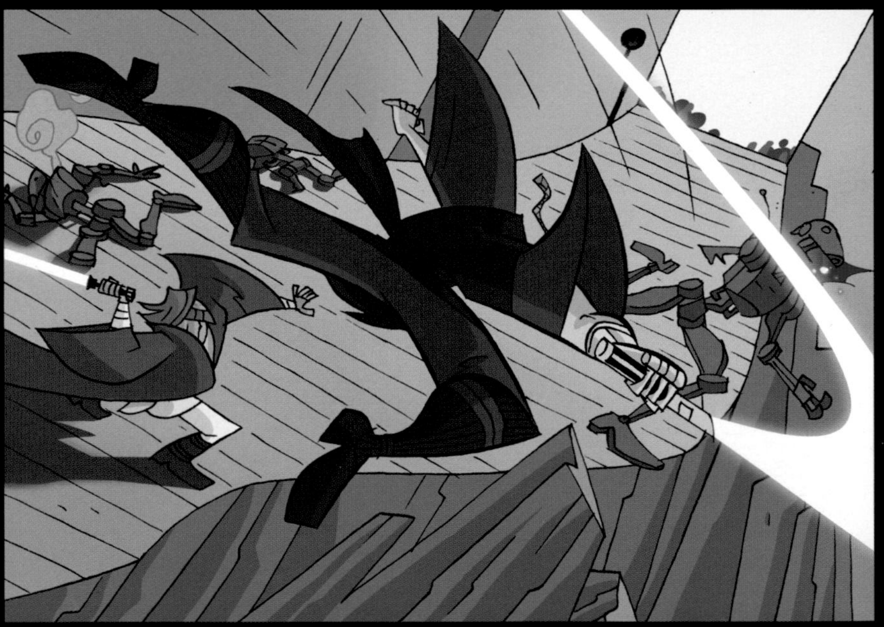

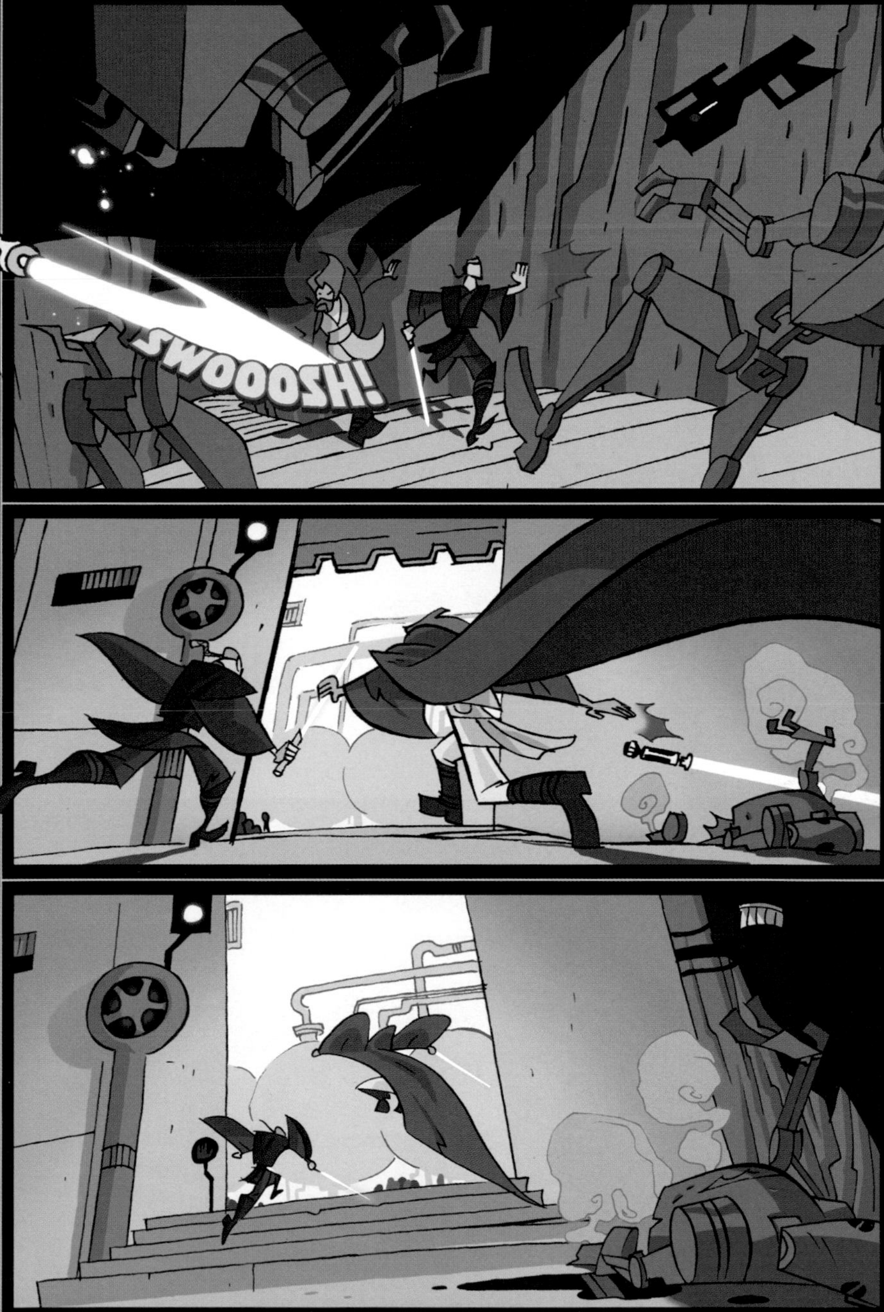
SWOOOSH!

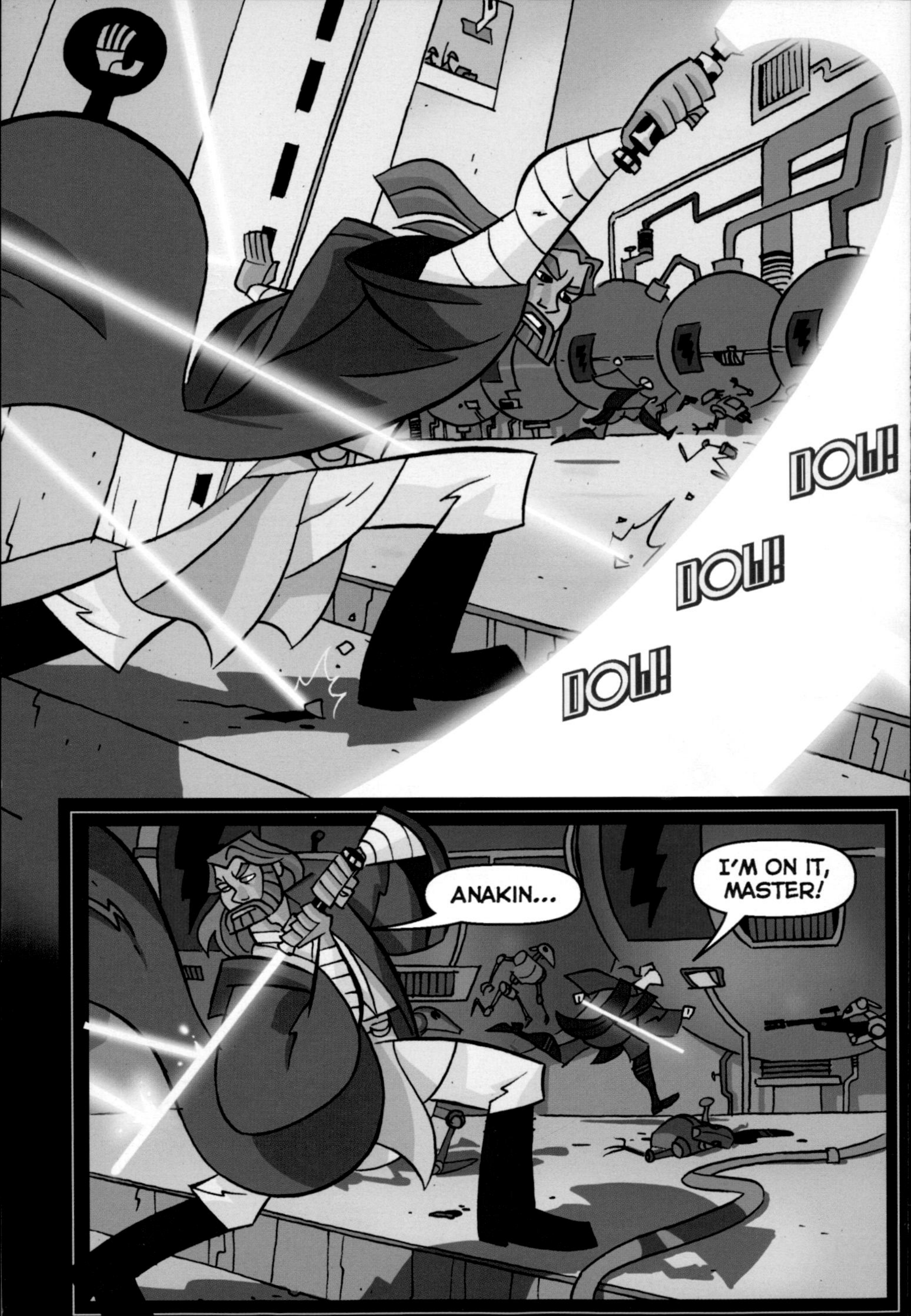
DOW!
DOW!
DOW!
ANAKIN...
I'M ON IT, MASTER!

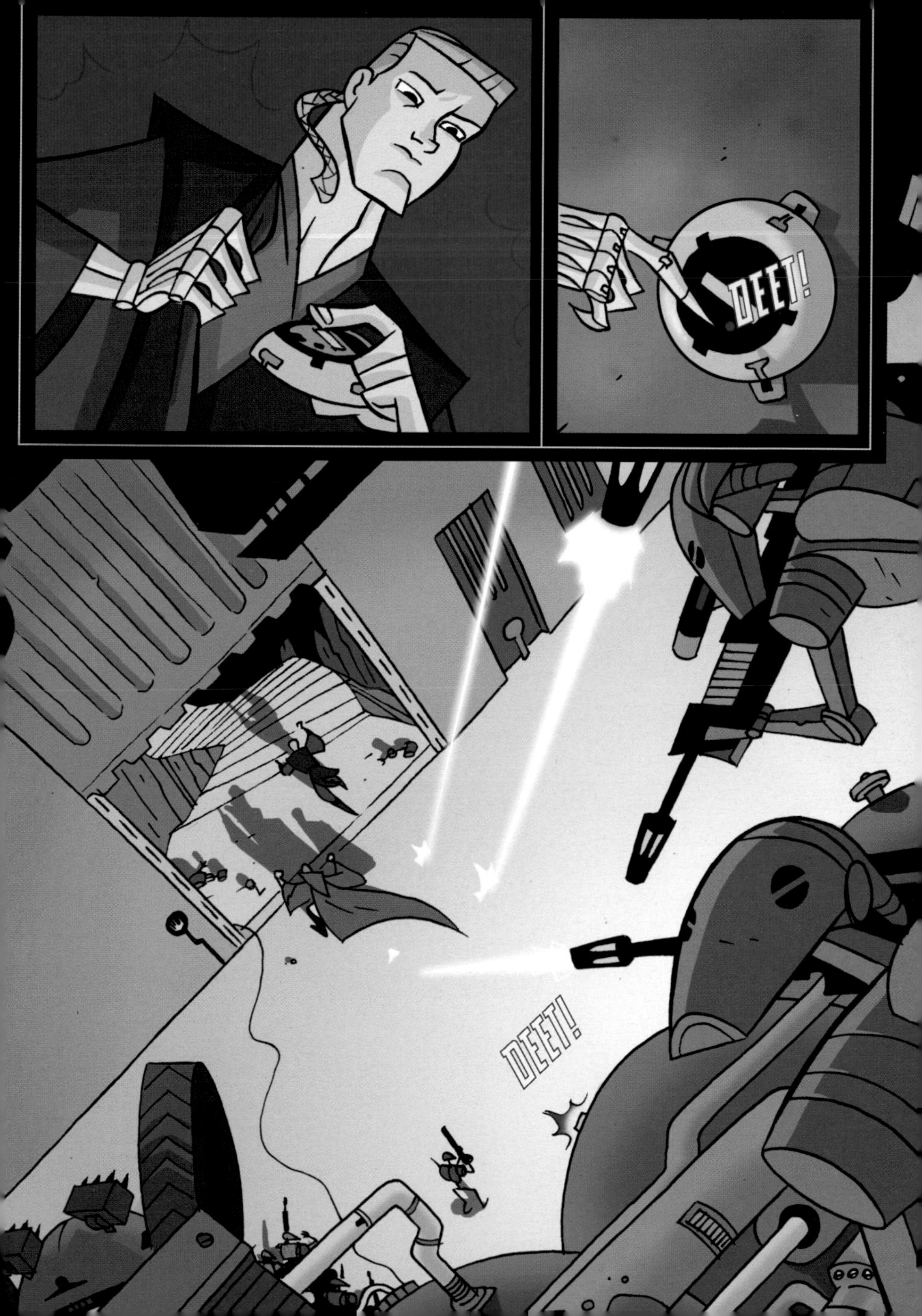
DEET!
DEET!

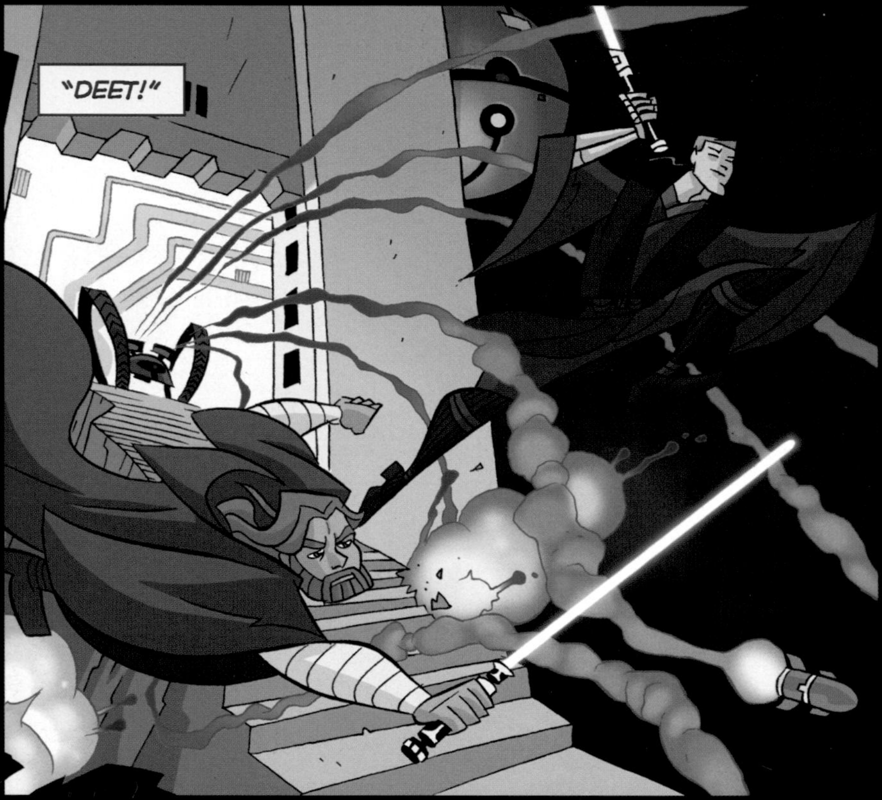
"DEET!"

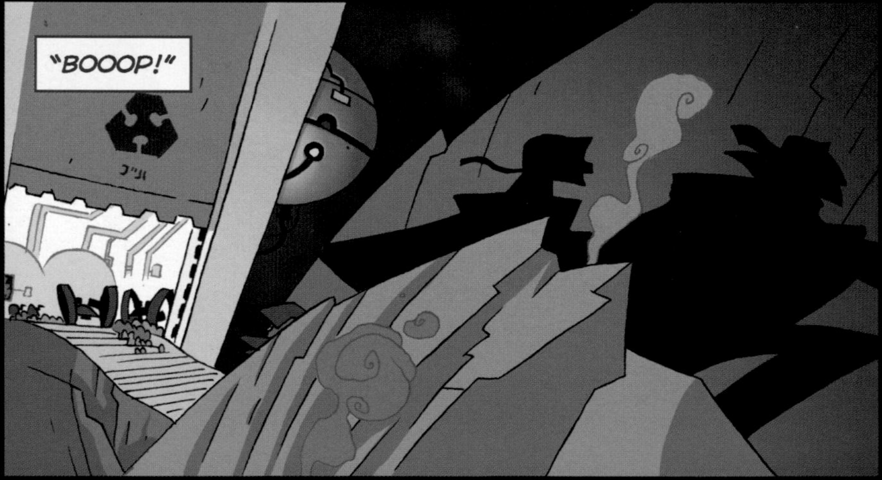
"BOOOP!"

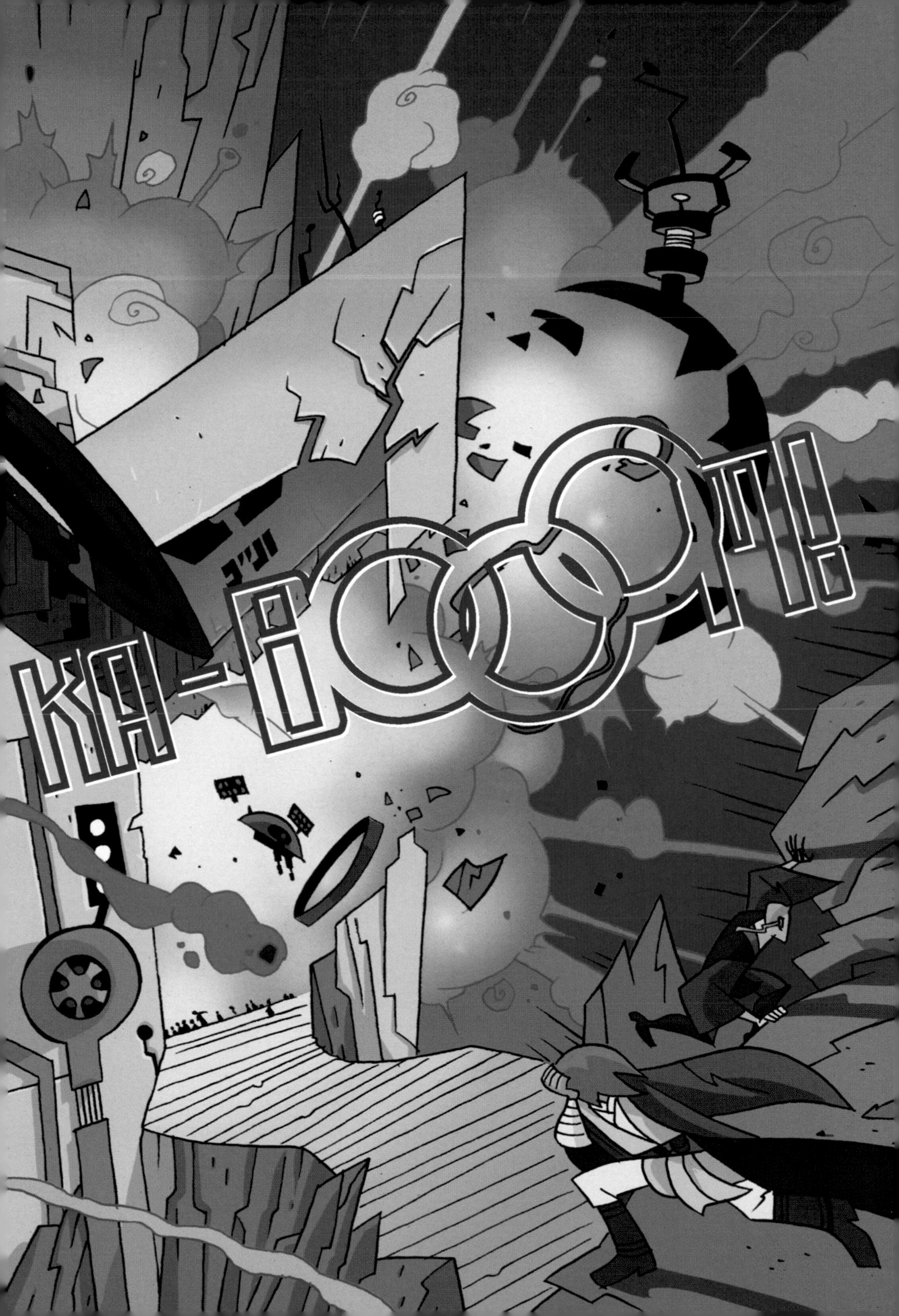
KA-BOOOM!

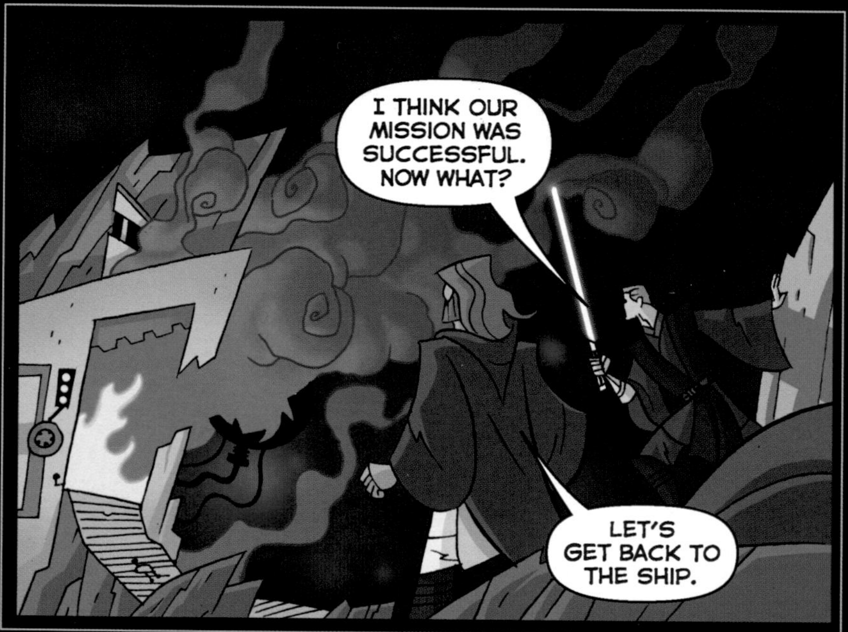
I THINK OUR MISSION WAS SUCCESSFUL. NOW WHAT?
LET'S GET BACK TO THE SHIP.

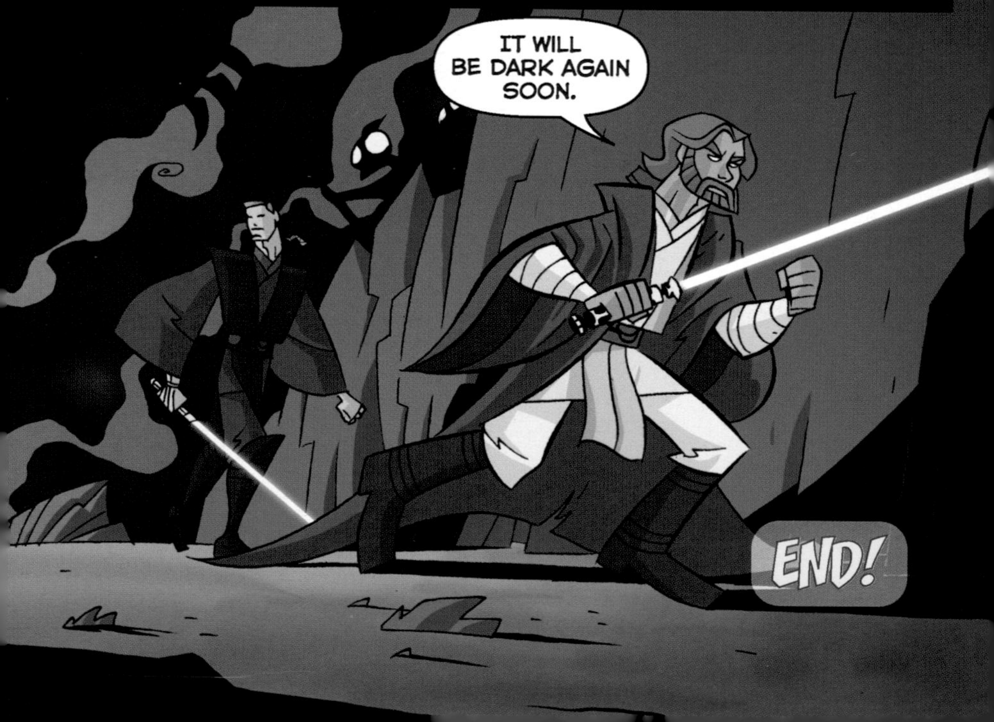
IT WILL BE DARK AGAIN SOON.
END!

STAR WARS
CLONE WARS
ADVENTURES

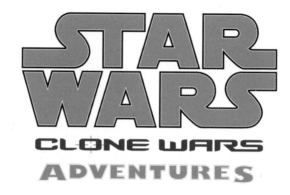

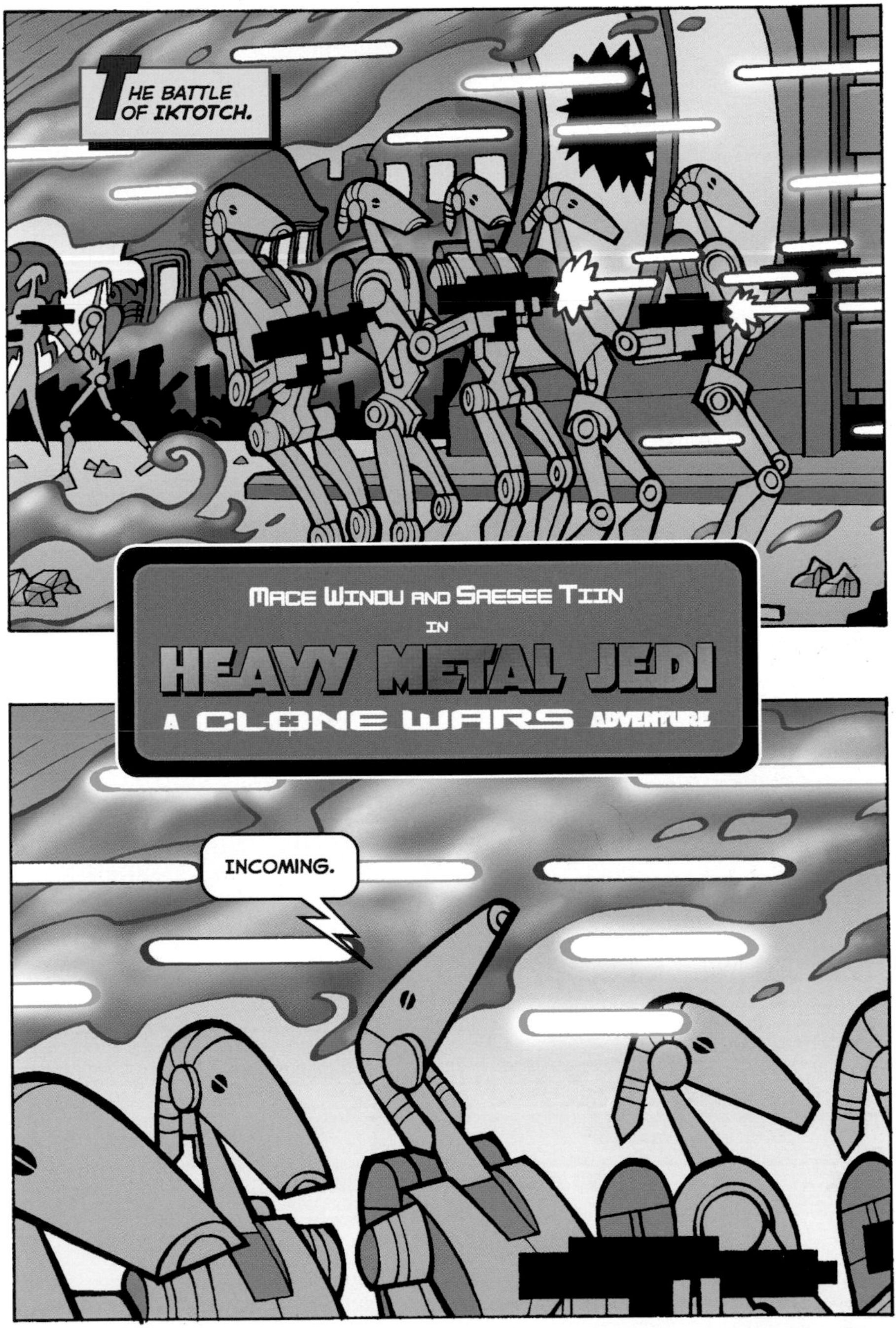
THE BATTLE OF IKTOTCH.
MACE WINDU AND SAESEE TIIN
IN
HEAVY METAL JEDI
A CLONE WARS ADVENTURE
INCOMING.

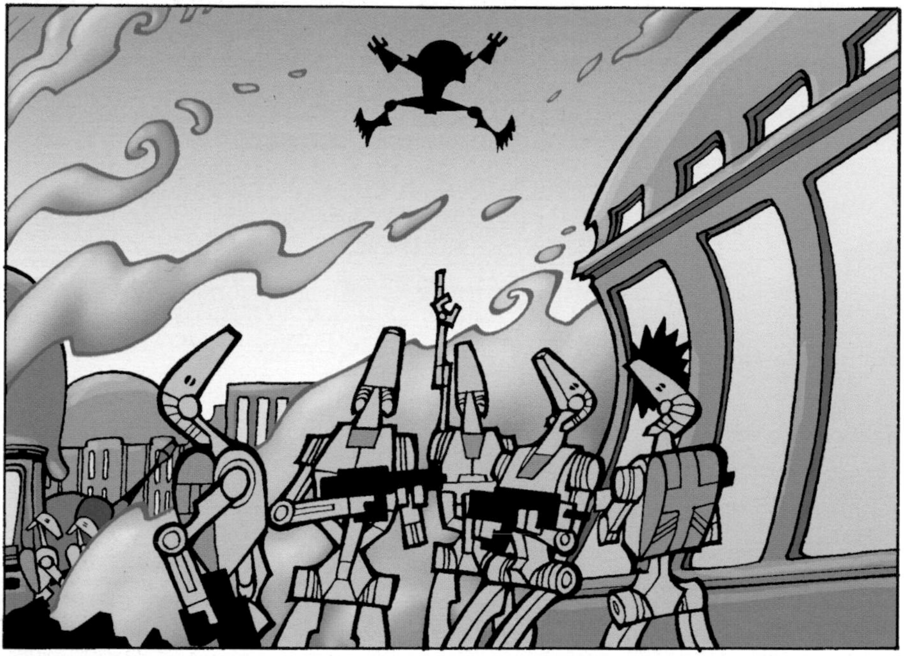

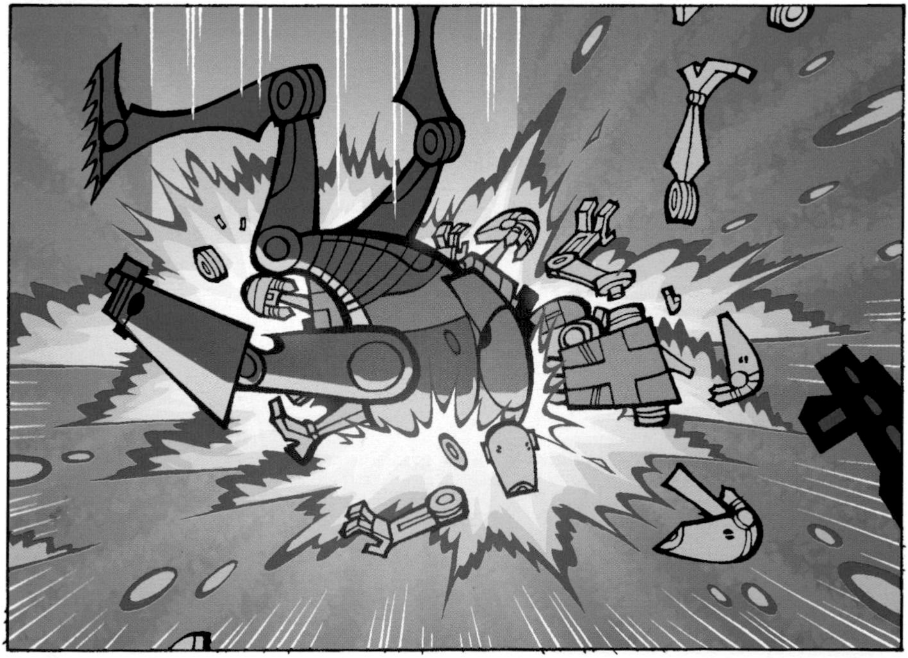

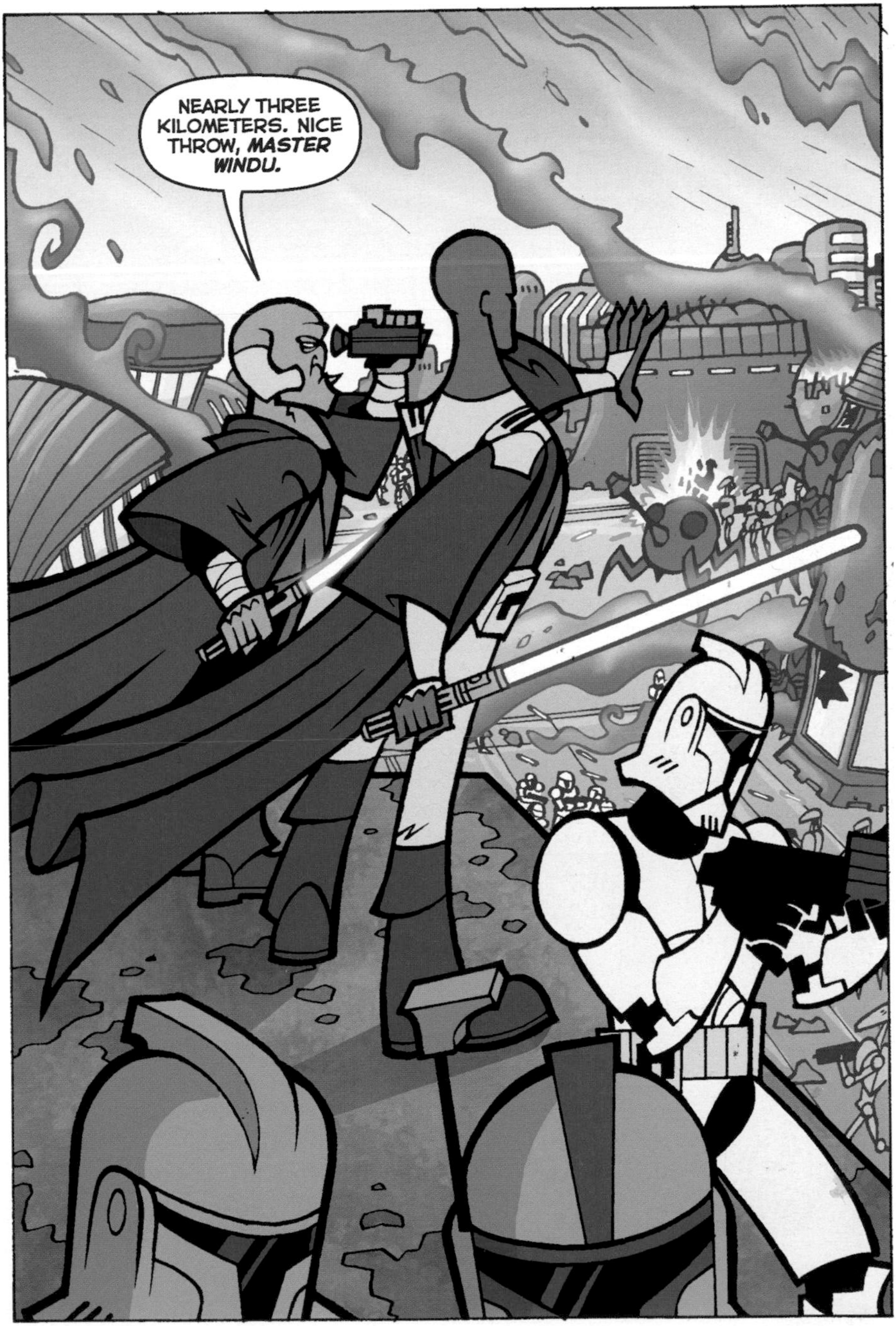
NEARLY THREE KILOMETERS. NICE THROW, *MASTER WINDU.*

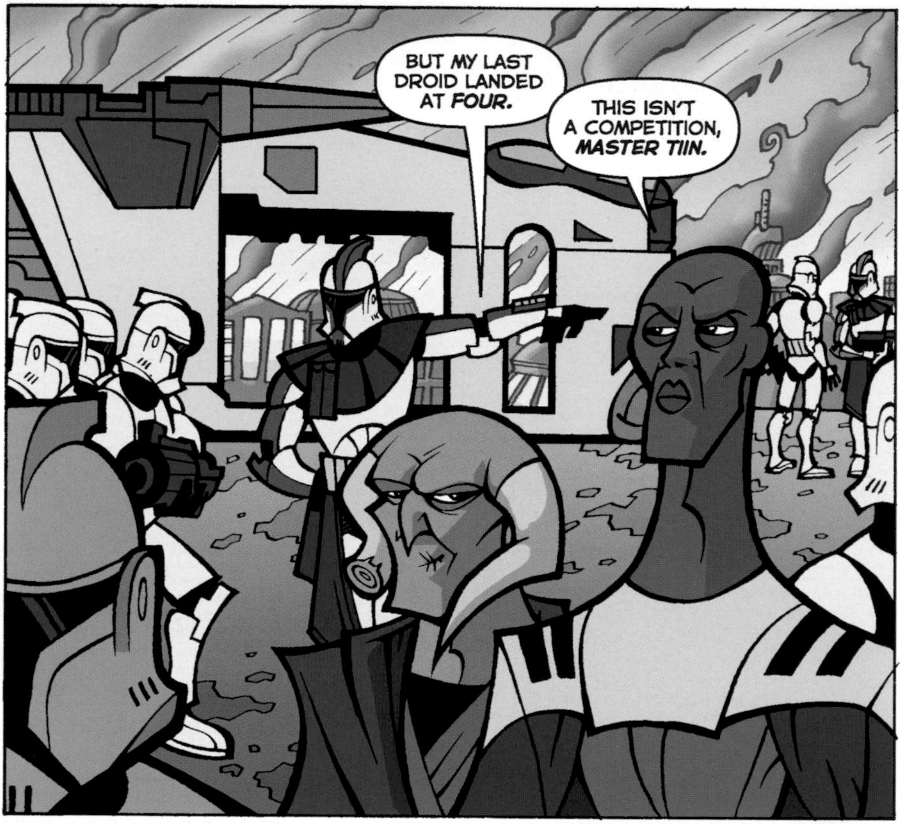
BUT MY LAST DROID LANDED AT FOUR.
THIS ISN'T A COMPETITION, MASTER TIIN.

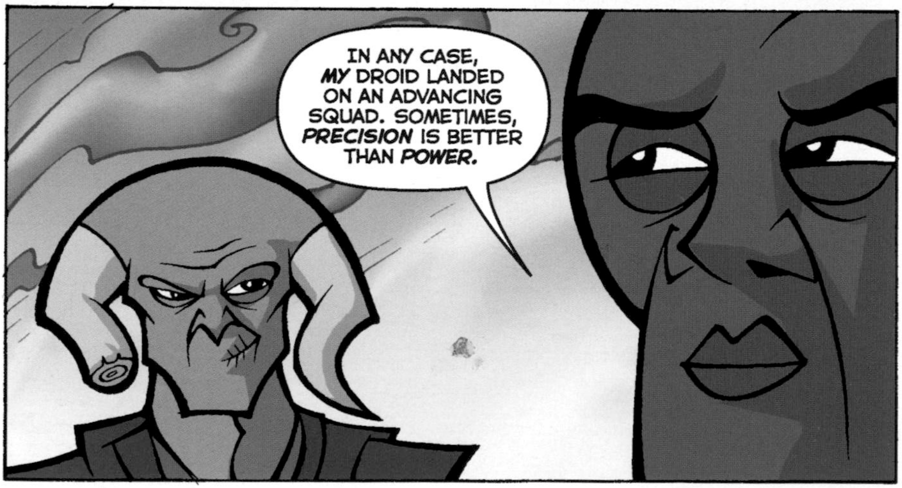
IN ANY CASE, MY DROID LANDED ON AN ADVANCING SQUAD. SOMETIMES, PRECISION IS BETTER THAN POWER.

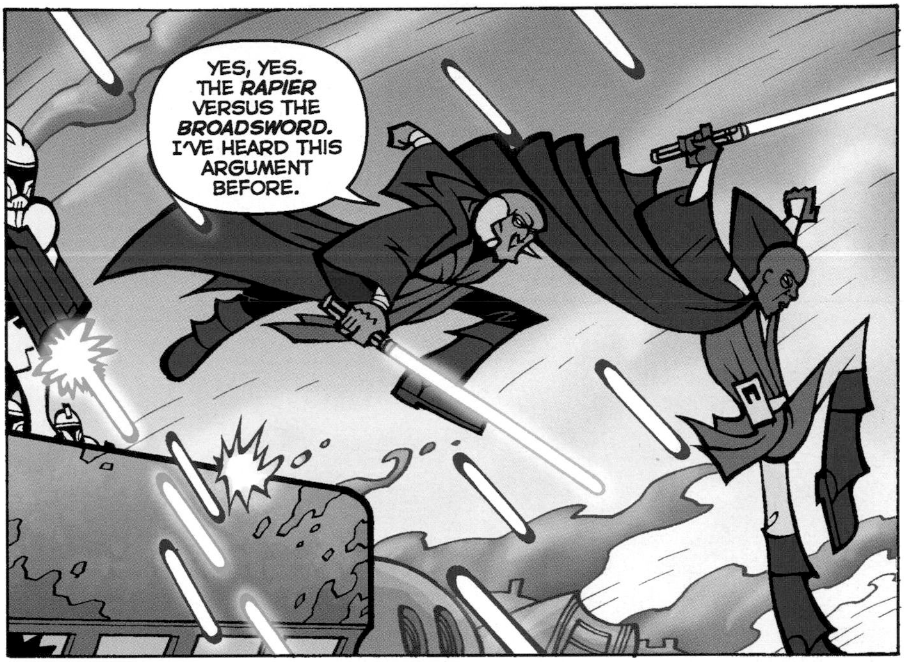
YES, YES. THE *RAPIER* VERSUS THE *BROADSWORD.* I'VE HEARD THIS ARGUMENT BEFORE.

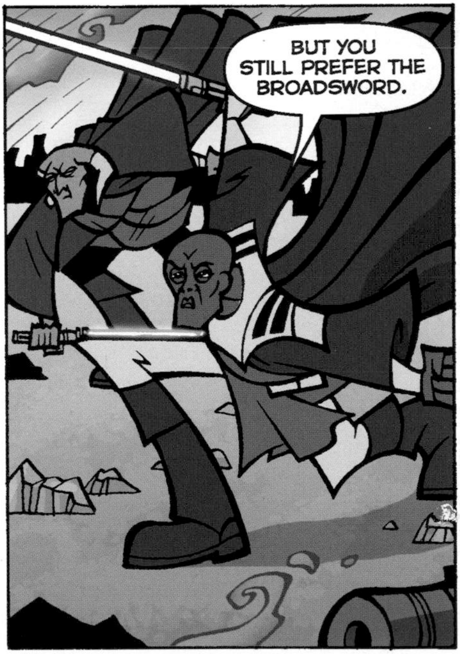
BUT YOU STILL PREFER THE BROADSWORD.

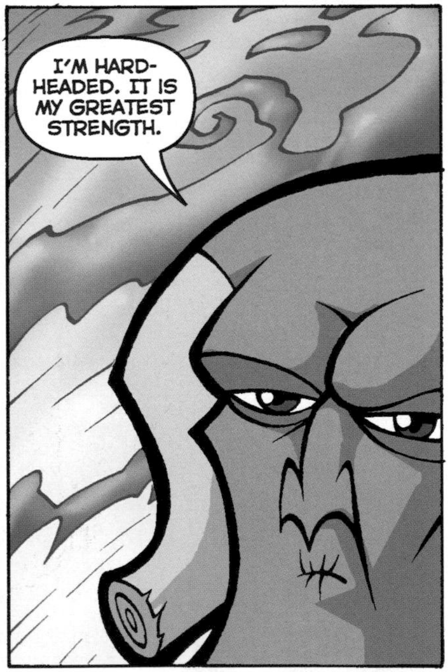
I'M HARD-HEADED. IT IS MY GREATEST STRENGTH.

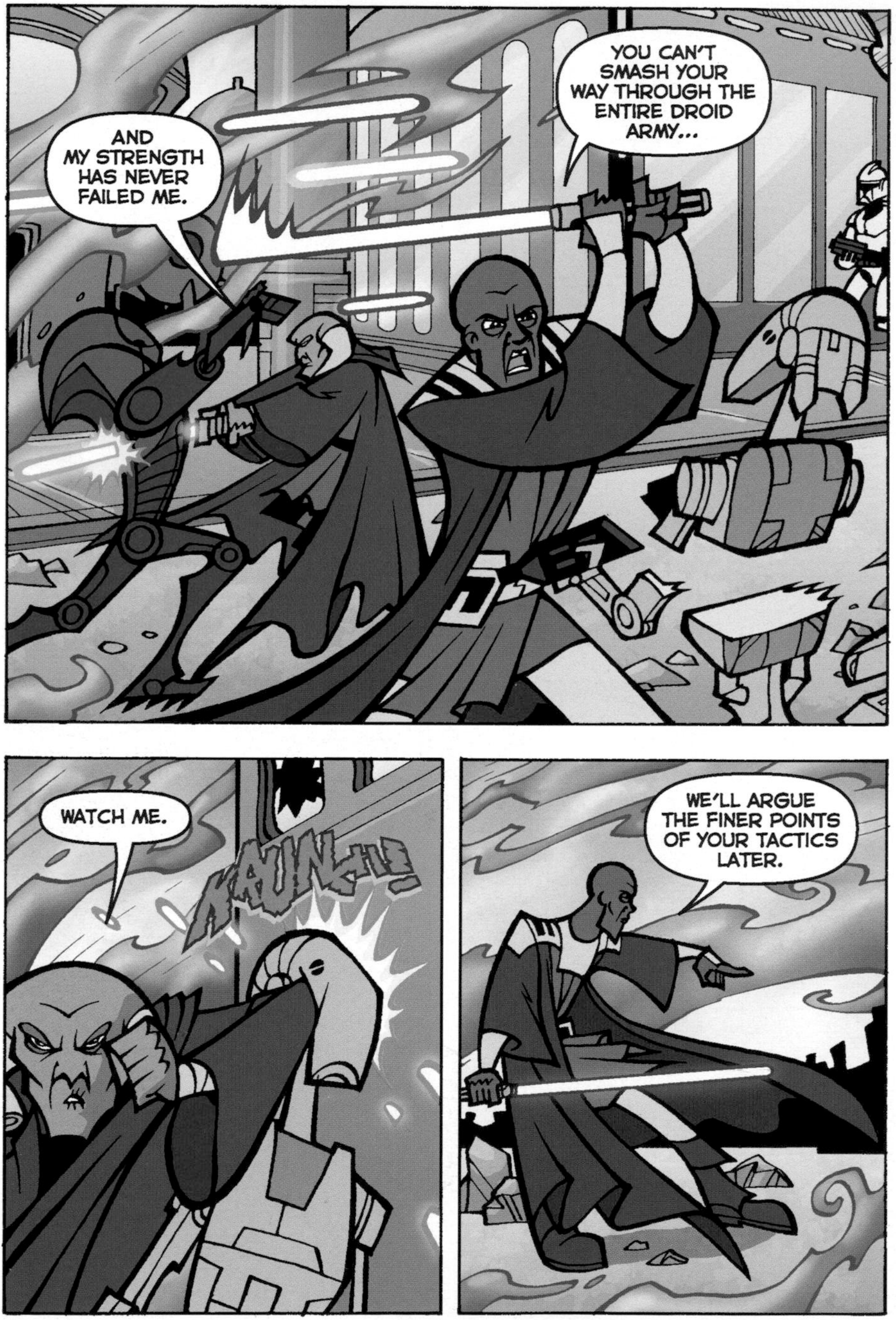
AND MY STRENGTH HAS NEVER FAILED ME.
YOU CAN'T SMASH YOUR WAY THROUGH THE ENTIRE DROID ARMY...
WATCH ME.
KAUNCH!
WE'LL ARGUE THE FINER POINTS OF YOUR TACTICS LATER.

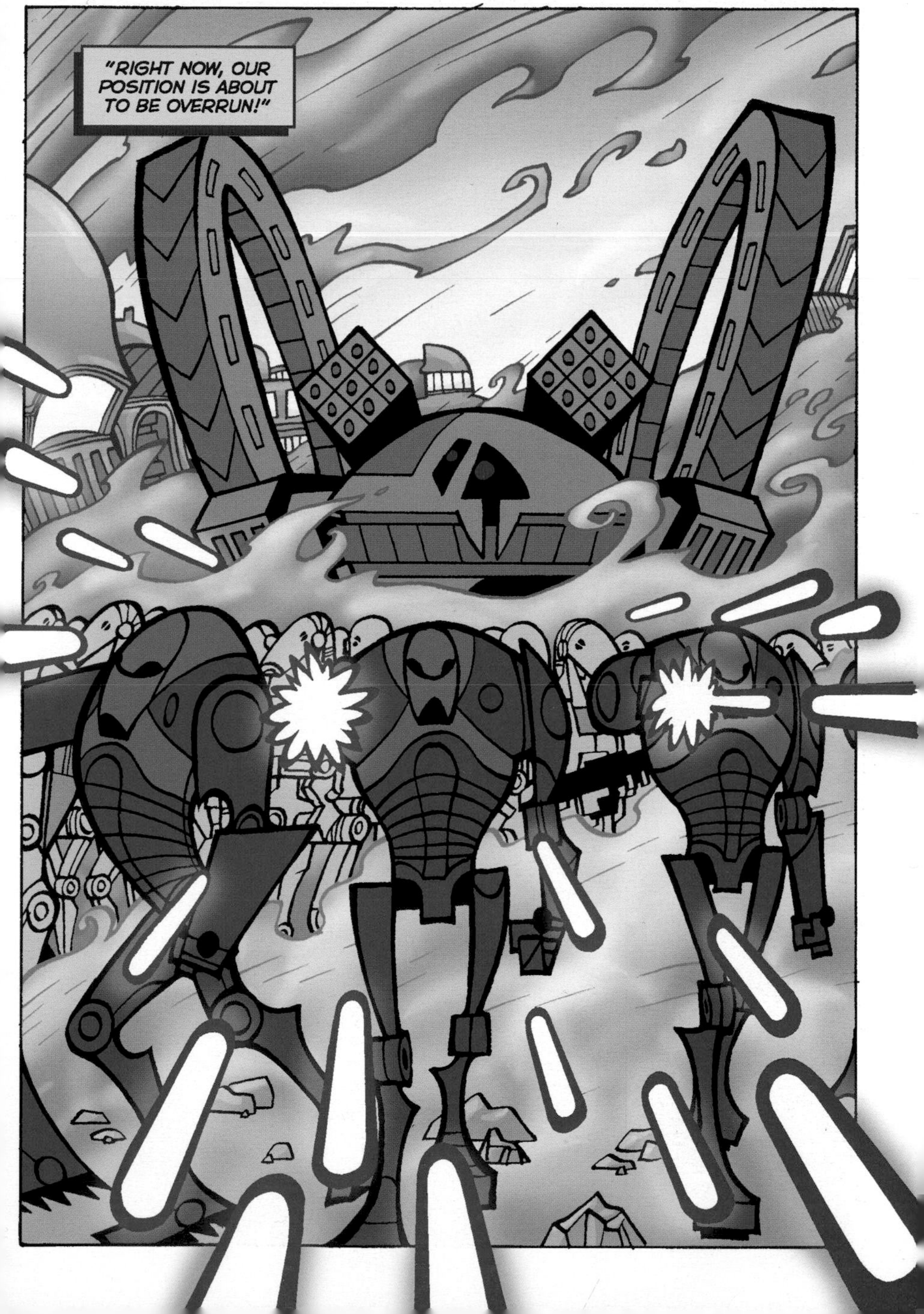
"RIGHT NOW, OUR POSITION IS ABOUT TO BE OVERRUN!"

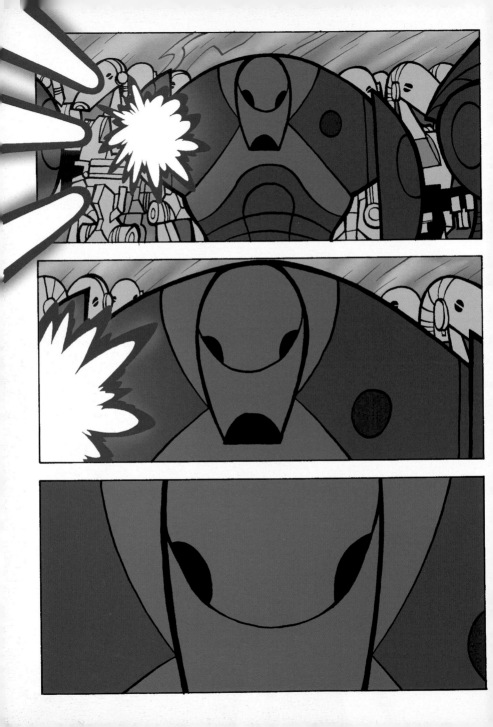

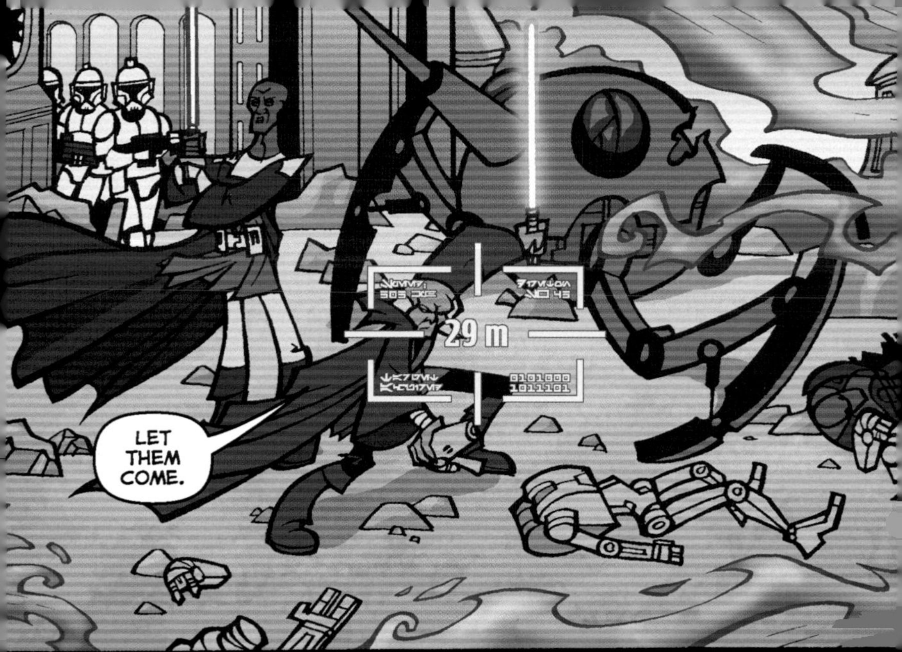
29 m
0101000
1011101
LET THEM COME.

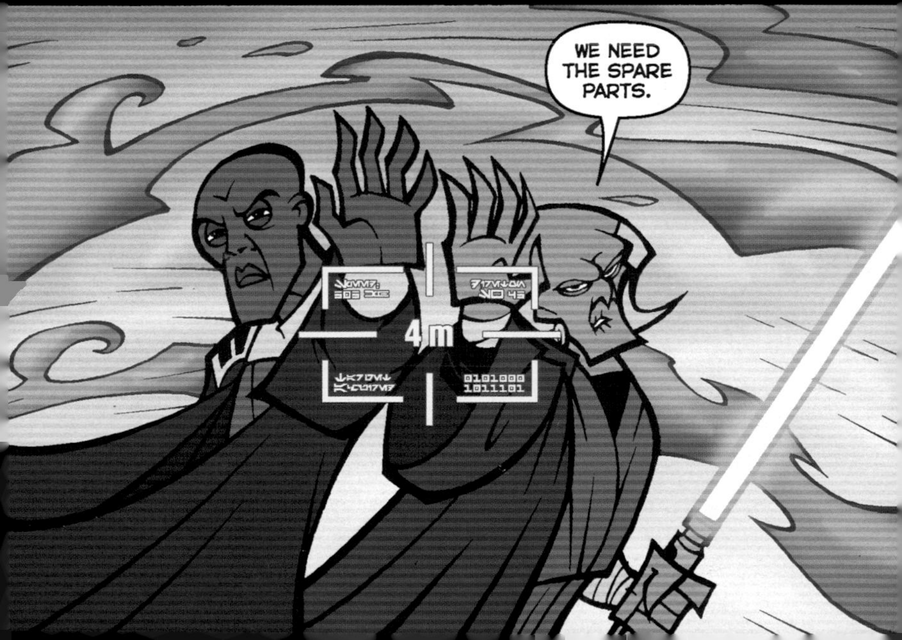
WE NEED THE SPARE PARTS.
4 m
0101000
1011101

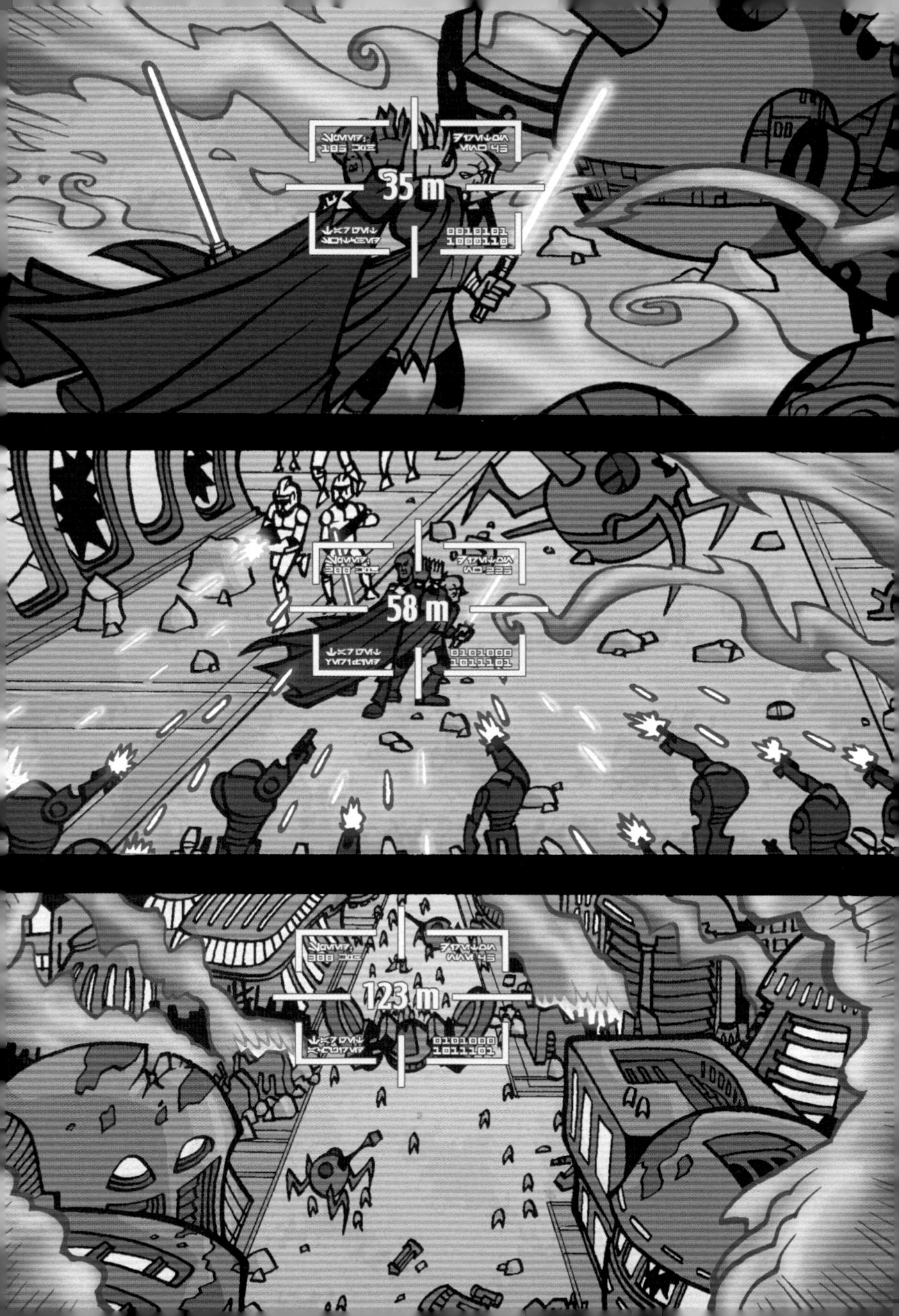
35 m
0010101
1000110
58 m
0101000
1011101
123 m
0101000
1011101

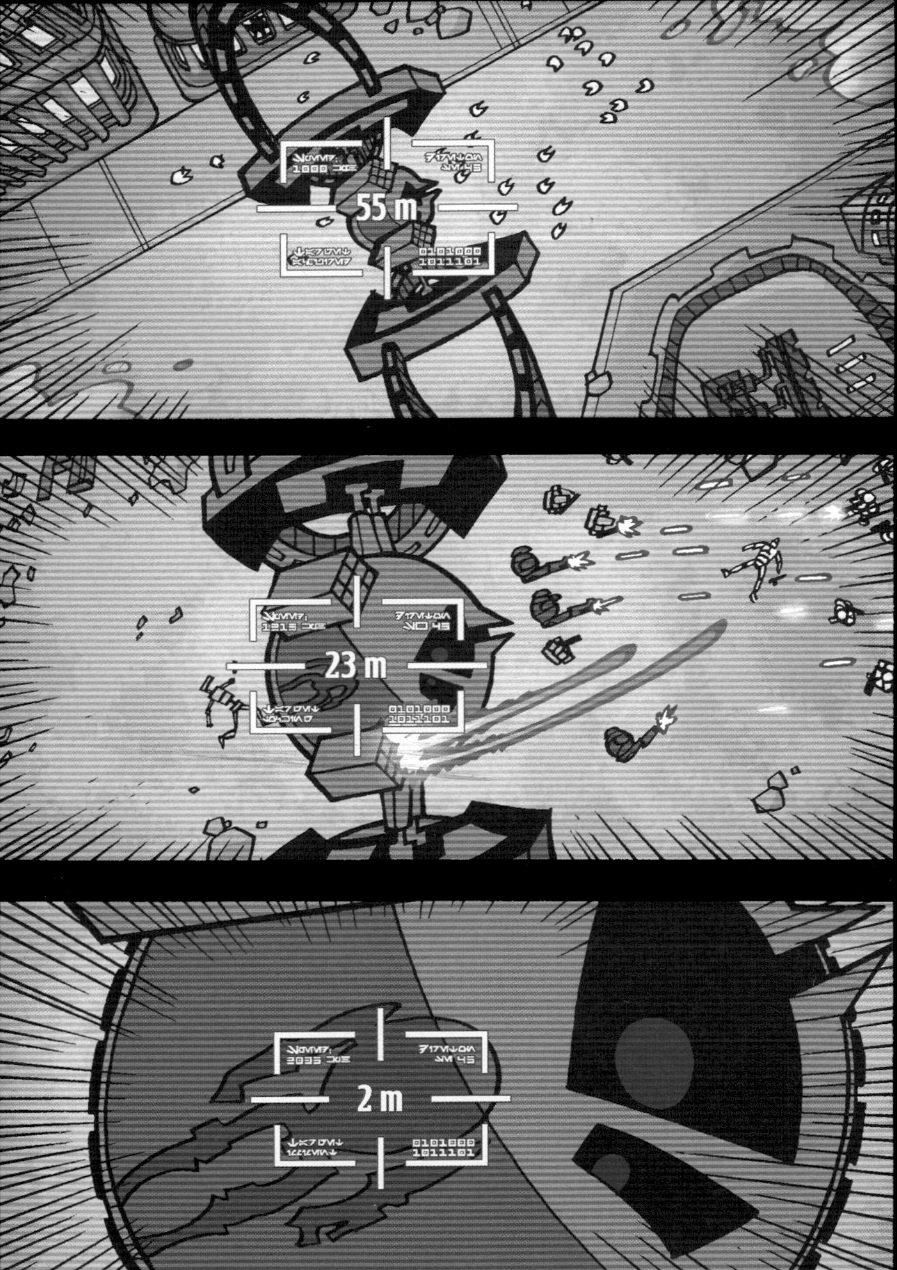

55 m
0101000
1011101
23 m
0101000
1011101
2 m
0101000
1011101

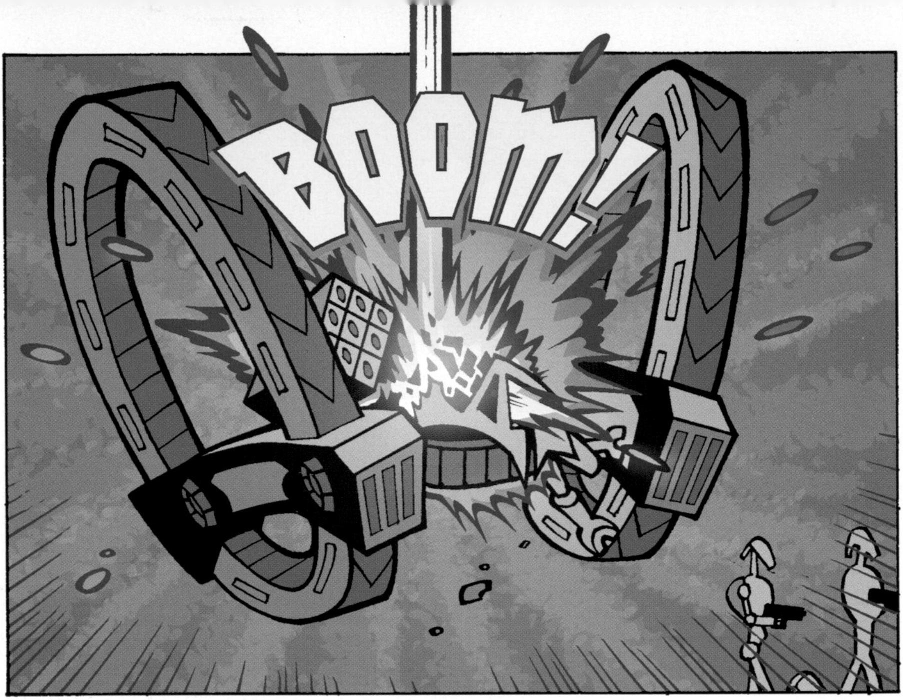
BOOM!

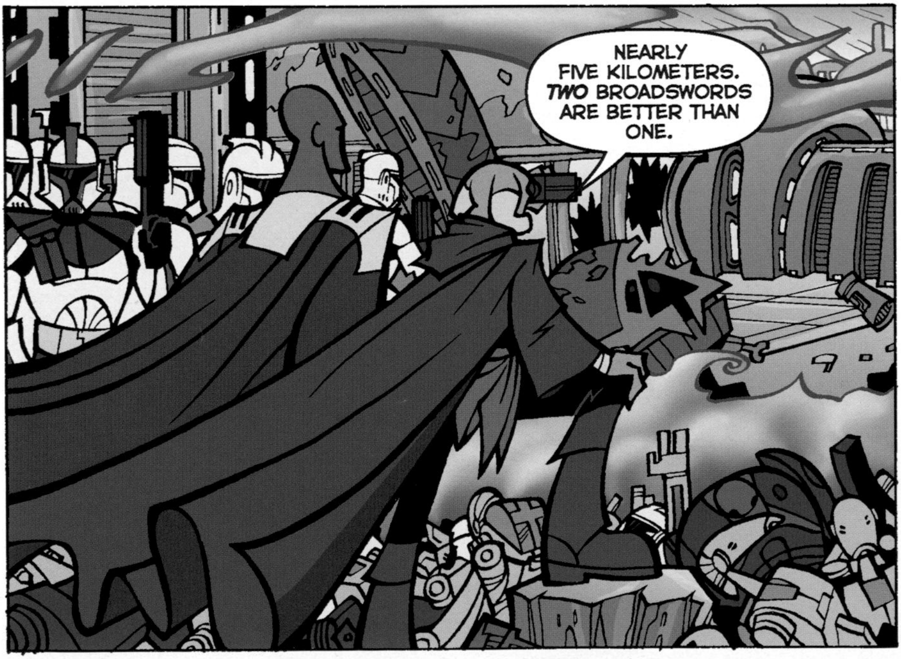
NEARLY FIVE KILOMETERS. *TWO* BROADSWORDS ARE BETTER THAN ONE.

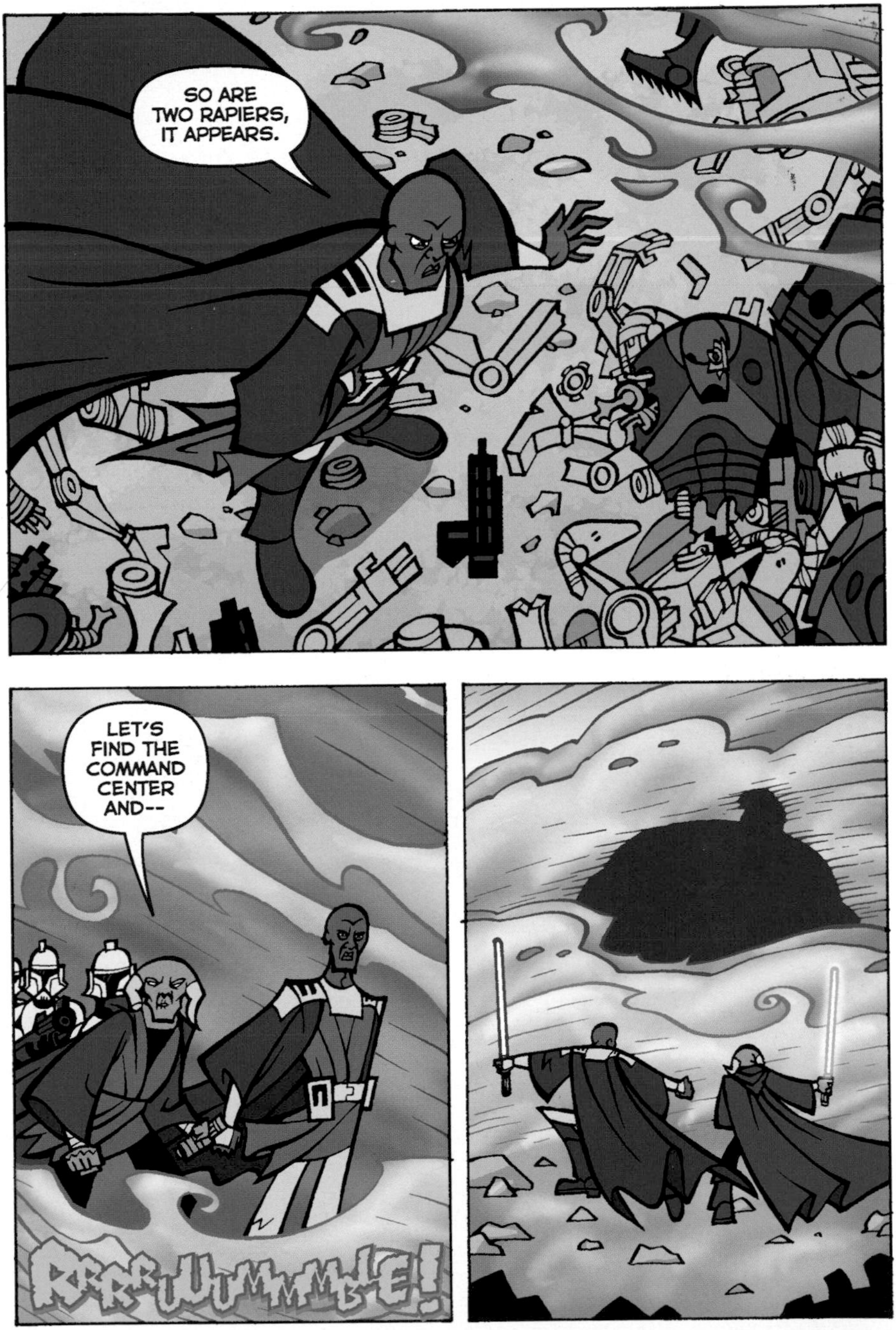
SO ARE TWO RAPIERS, IT APPEARS.
LET'S FIND THE COMMAND CENTER AND--
RRRRUUMMMBLE!

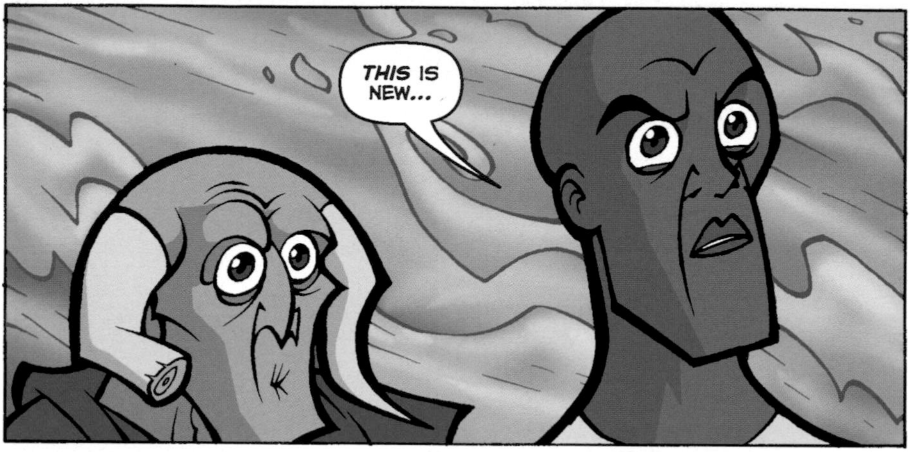
THIS IS NEW...

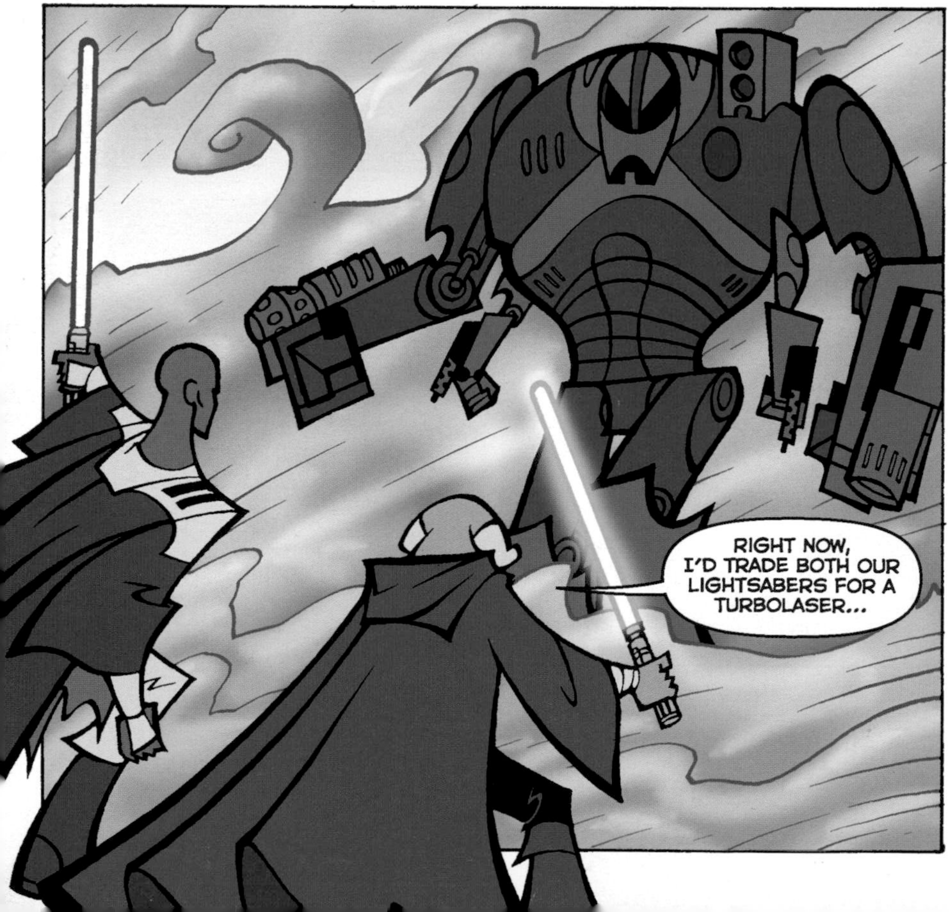
RIGHT NOW, I'D TRADE BOTH OUR LIGHTSABERS FOR A TURBOLASER...

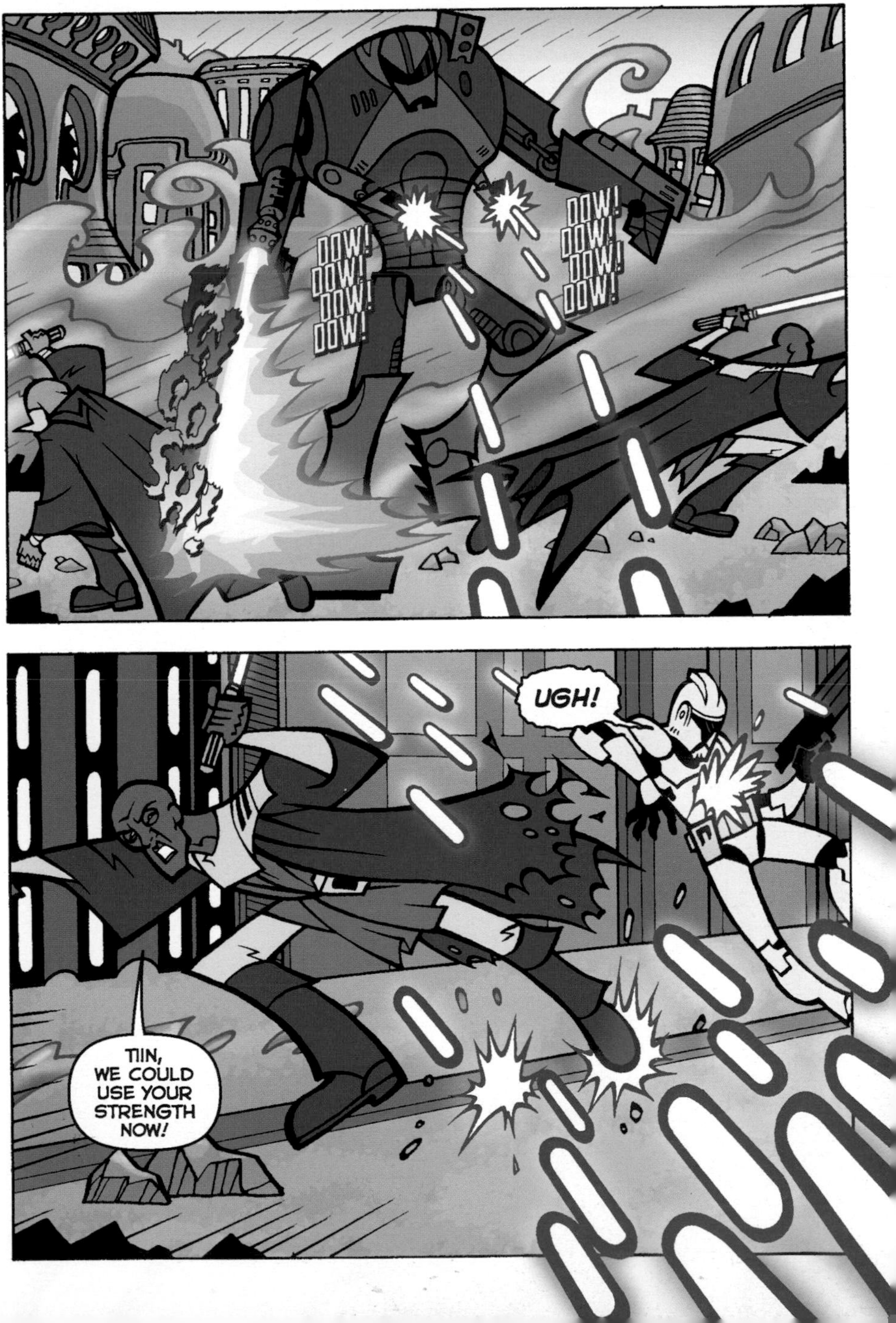
DOW! DOW! DOW! DOW!
DOW! DOW! DOW! DOW!
UGH!
TIIN, WE COULD USE YOUR STRENGTH NOW!

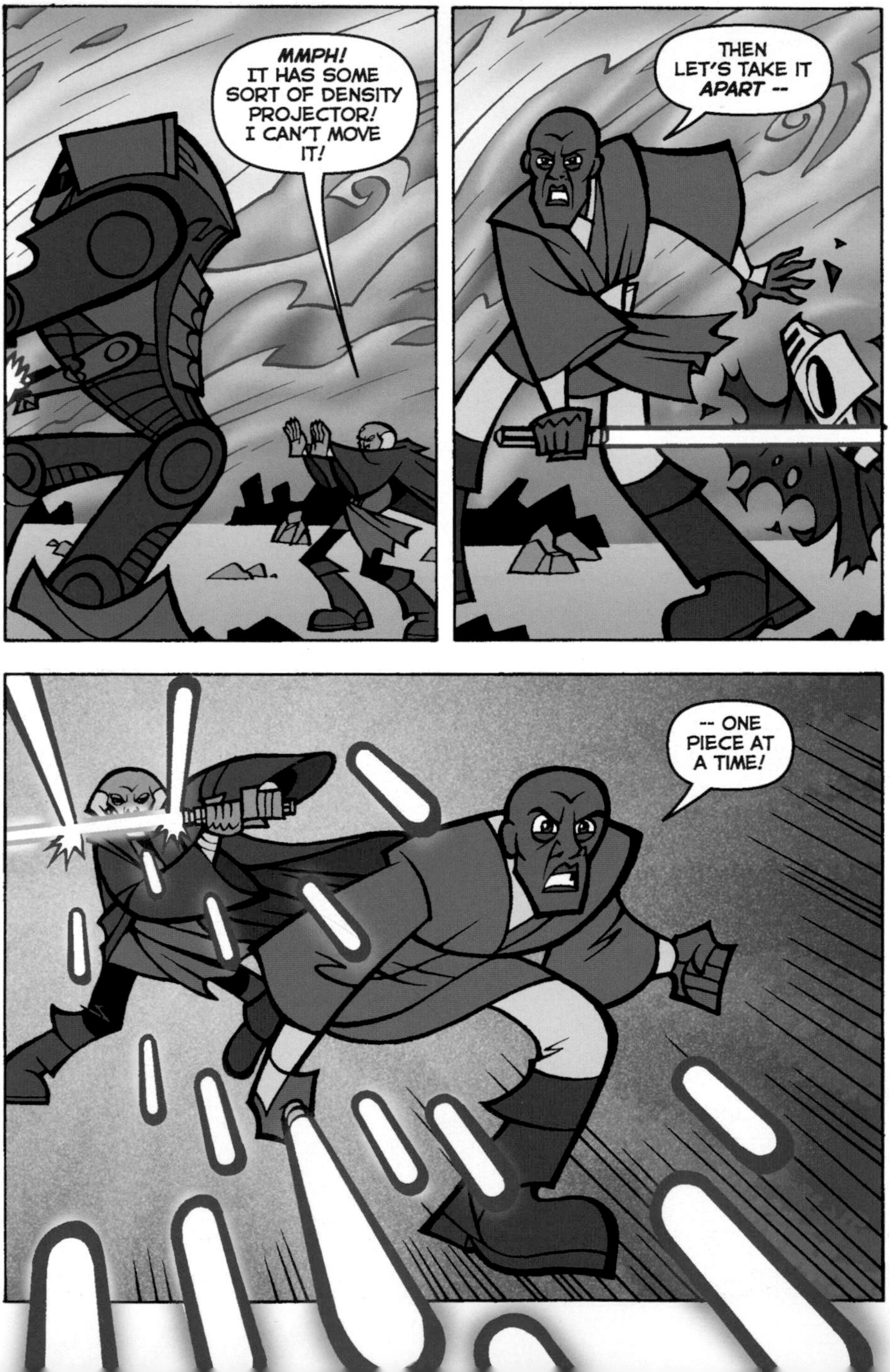
MMPH! IT HAS SOME SORT OF DENSITY PROJECTOR! I CAN'T MOVE IT!
THEN LET'S TAKE IT APART --
-- ONE PIECE AT A TIME!

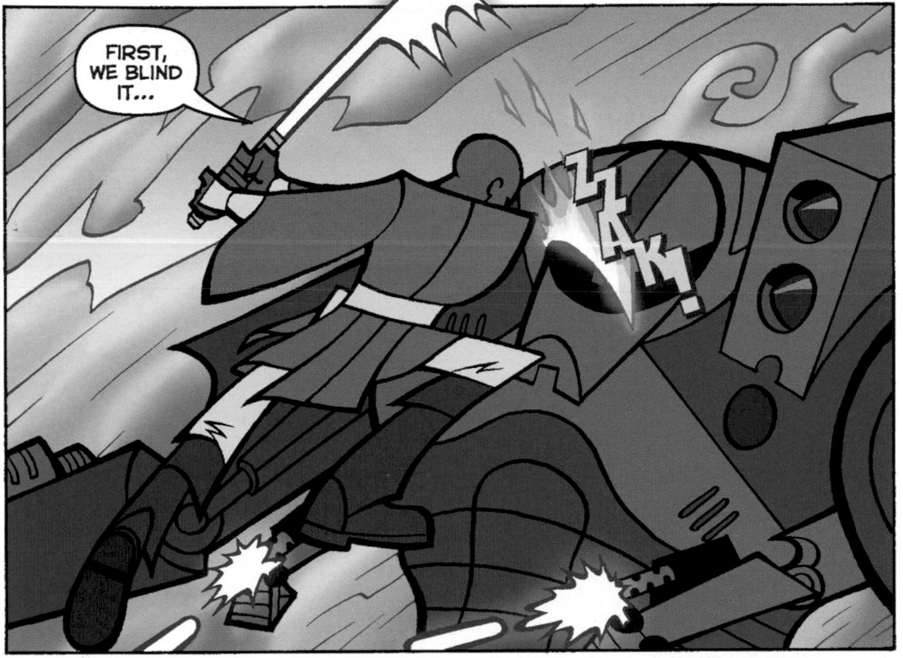
FIRST, WE BLIND IT...
ZZAAK!

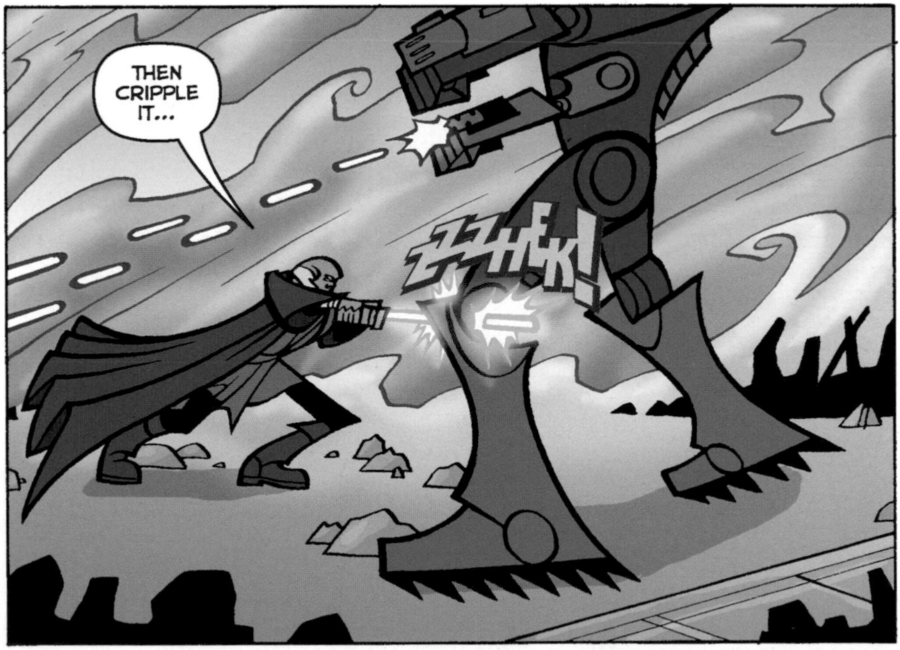
THEN CRIPPLE IT...
ZZHHEK!

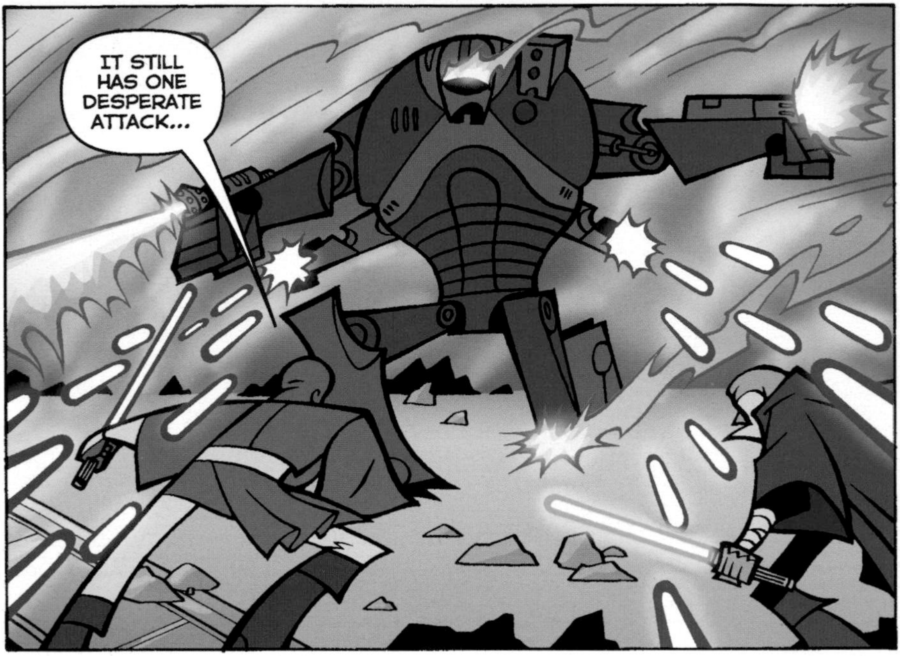
IT STILL HAS ONE DESPERATE ATTACK...

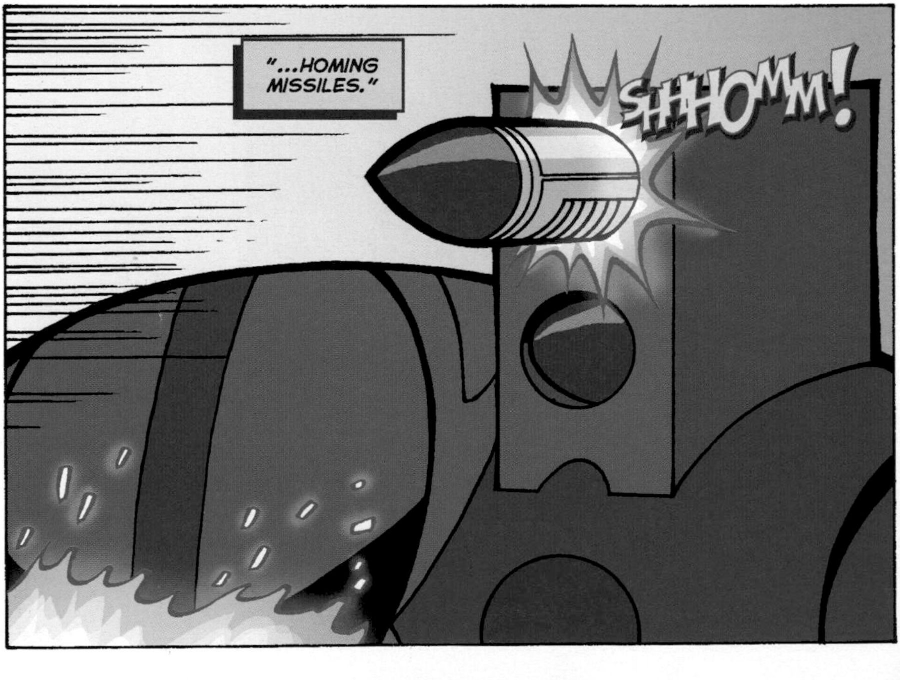
"...HOMING MISSILES."
SHHHOMMM!

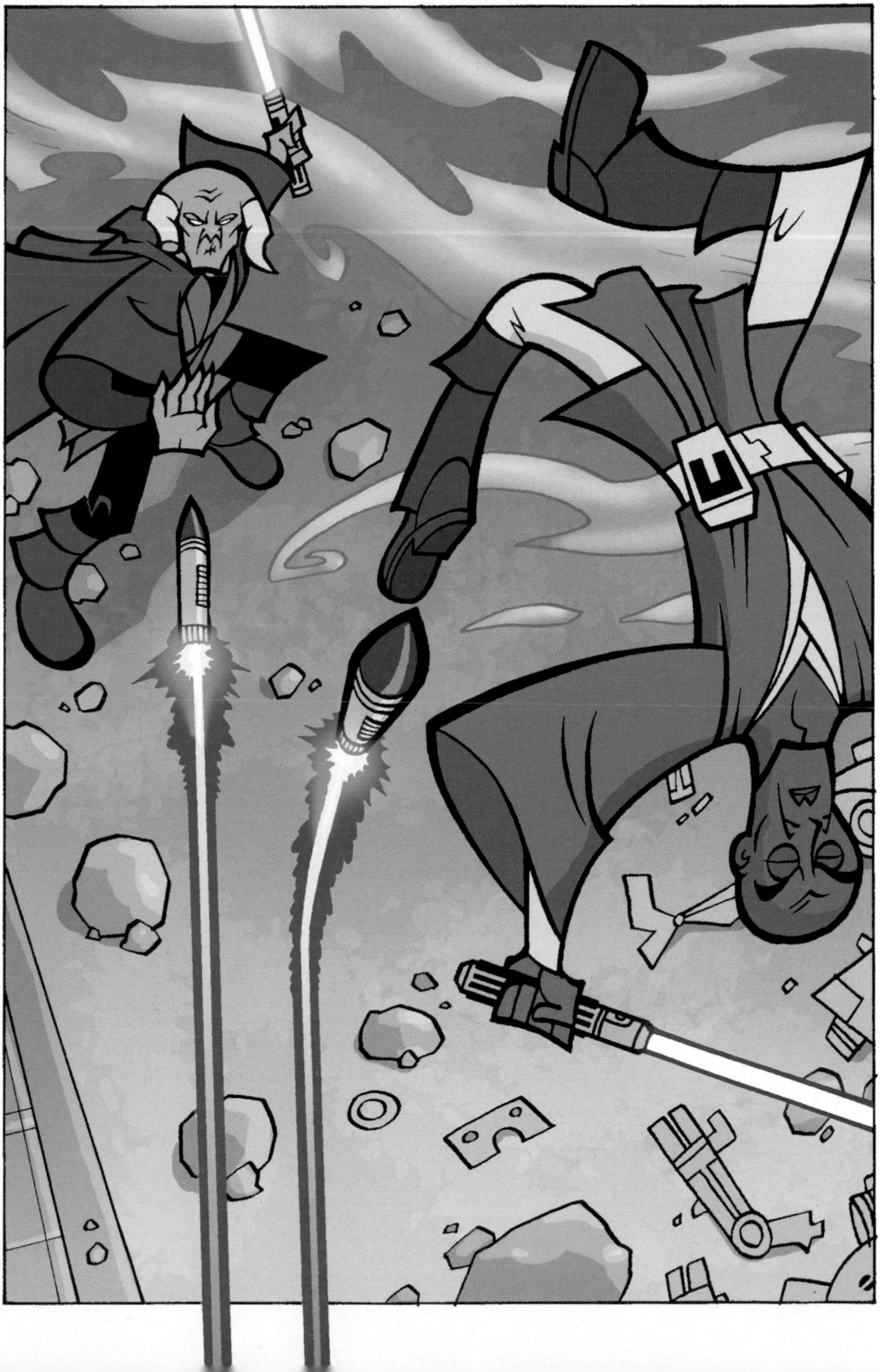

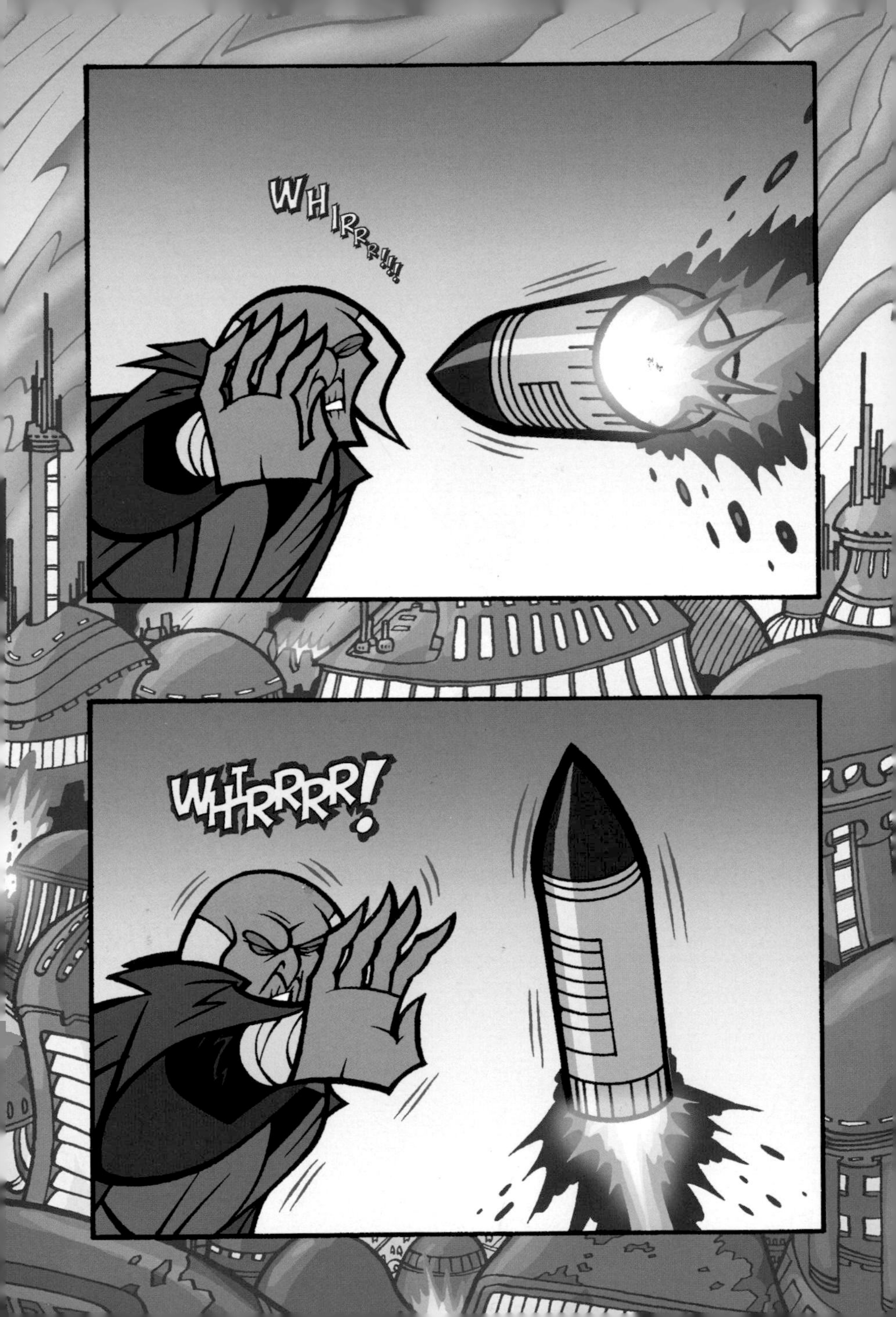
WHIRRR!!!
WHIRRRR!

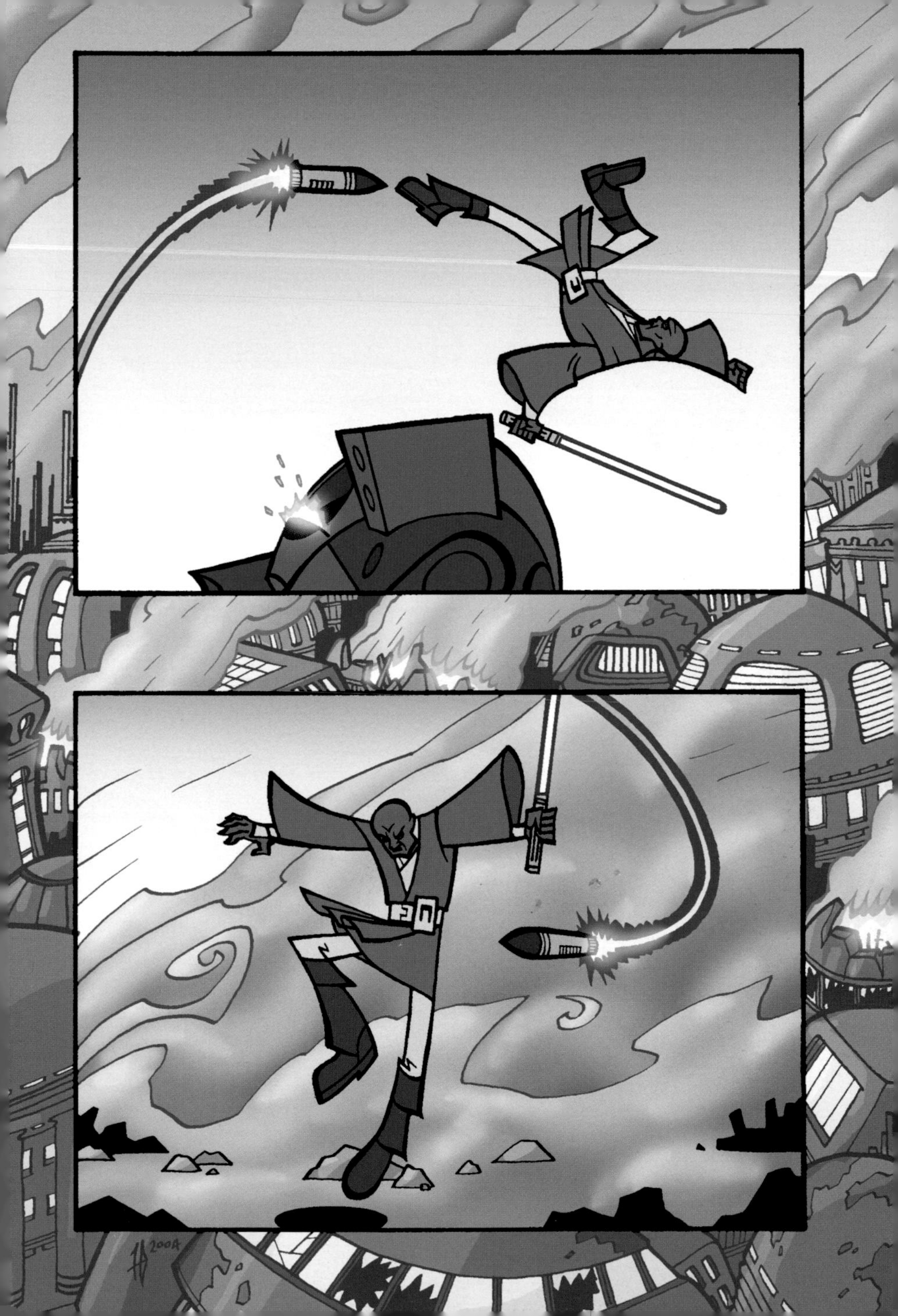

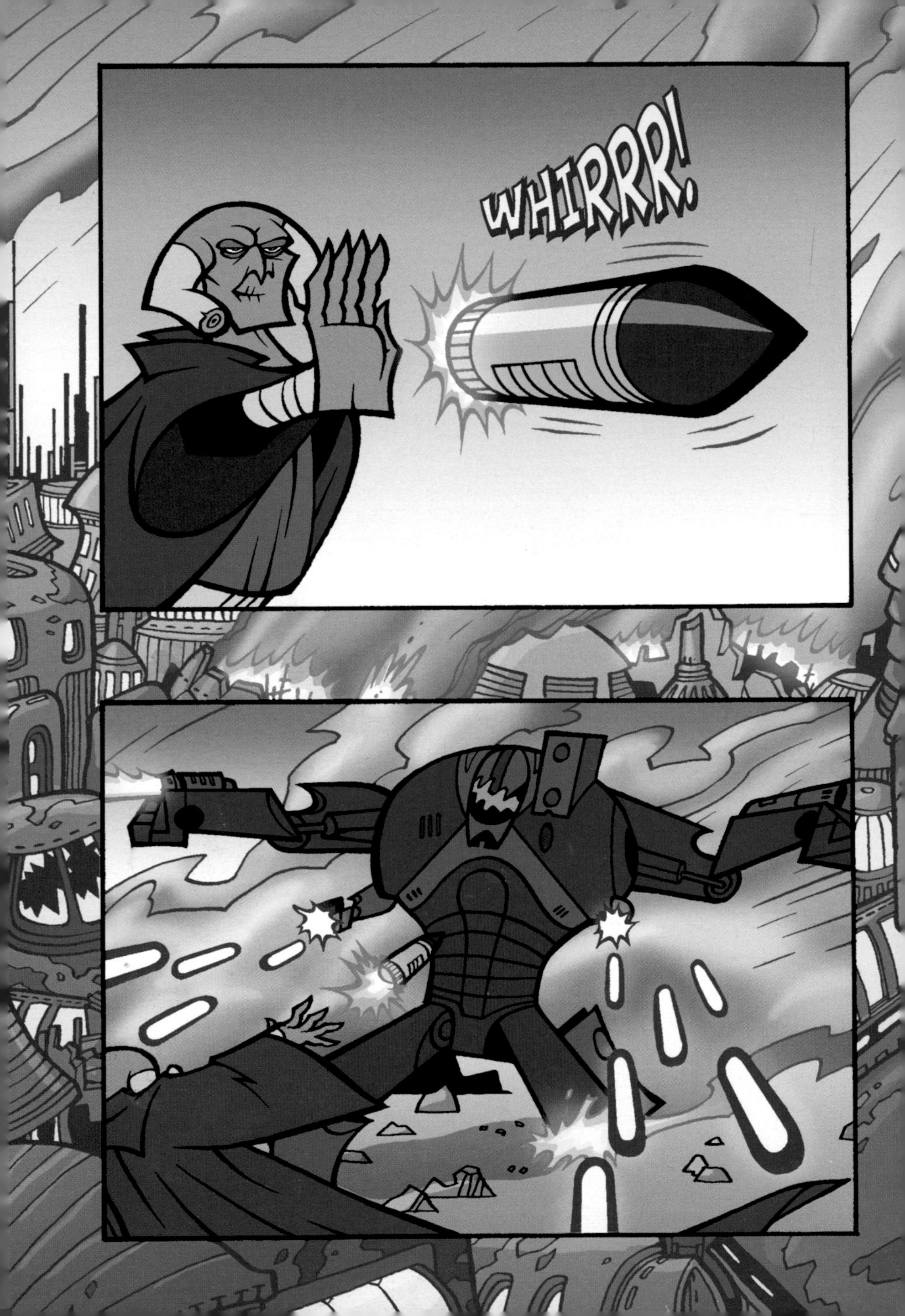
WHIRRR!

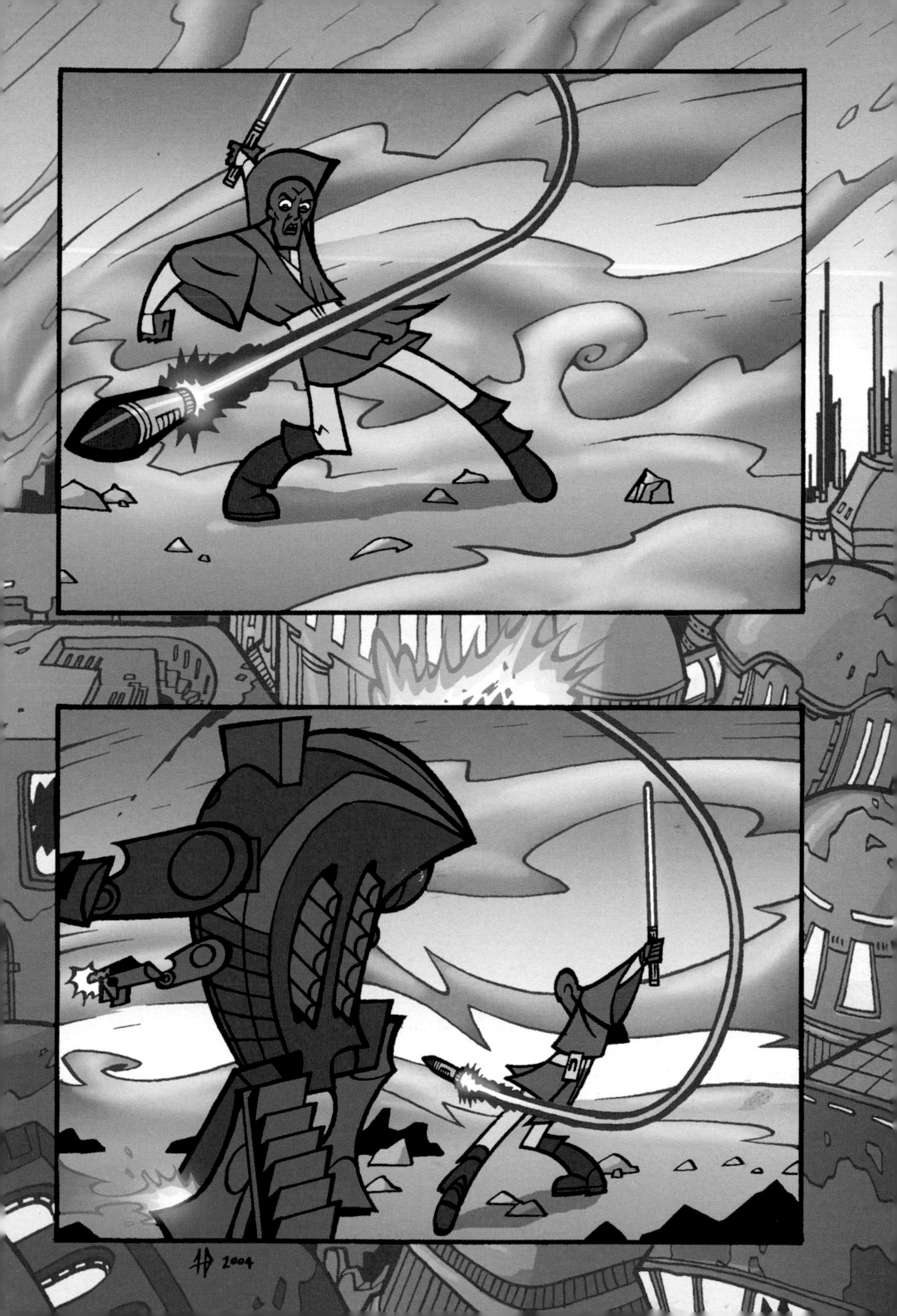
2004

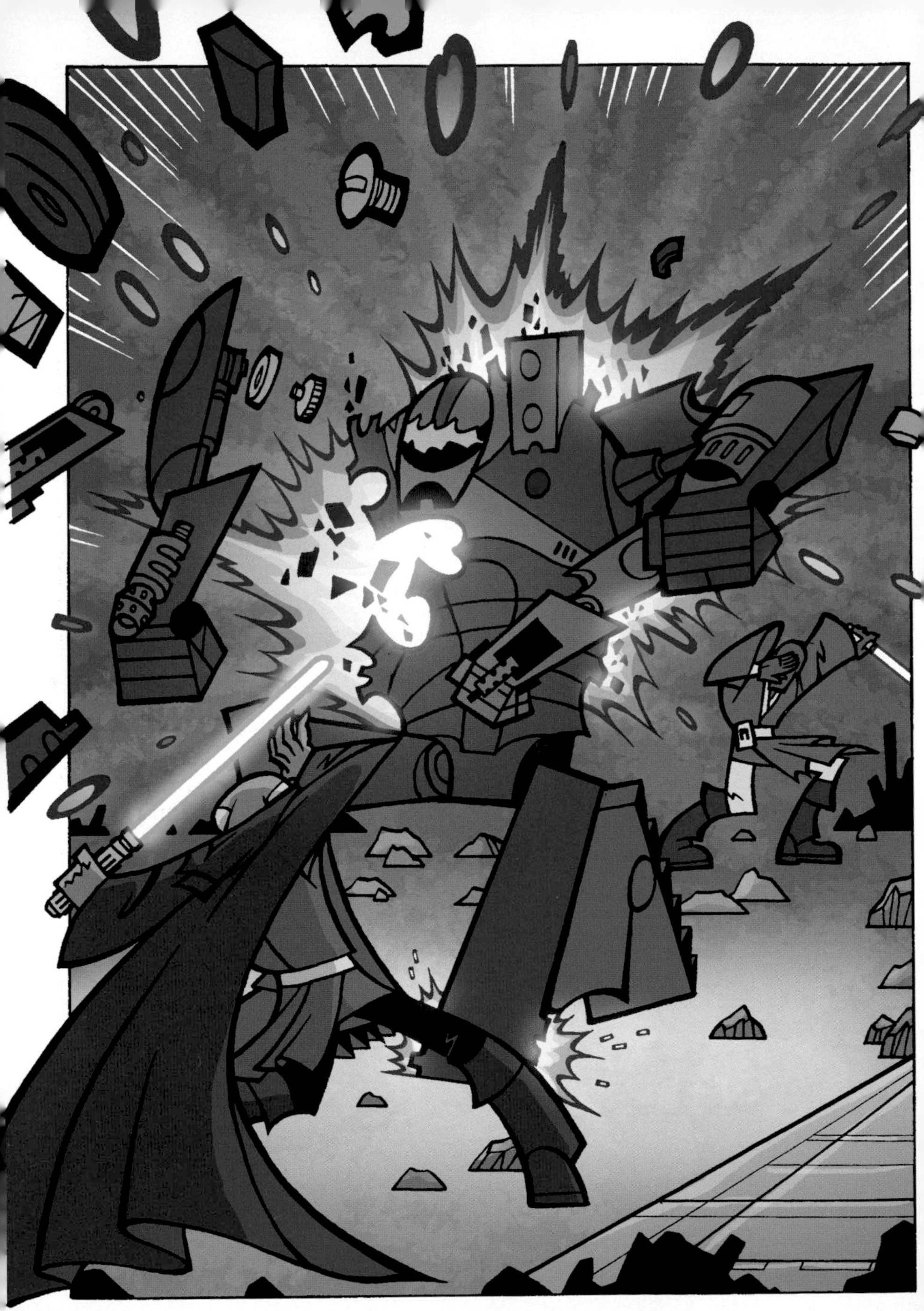

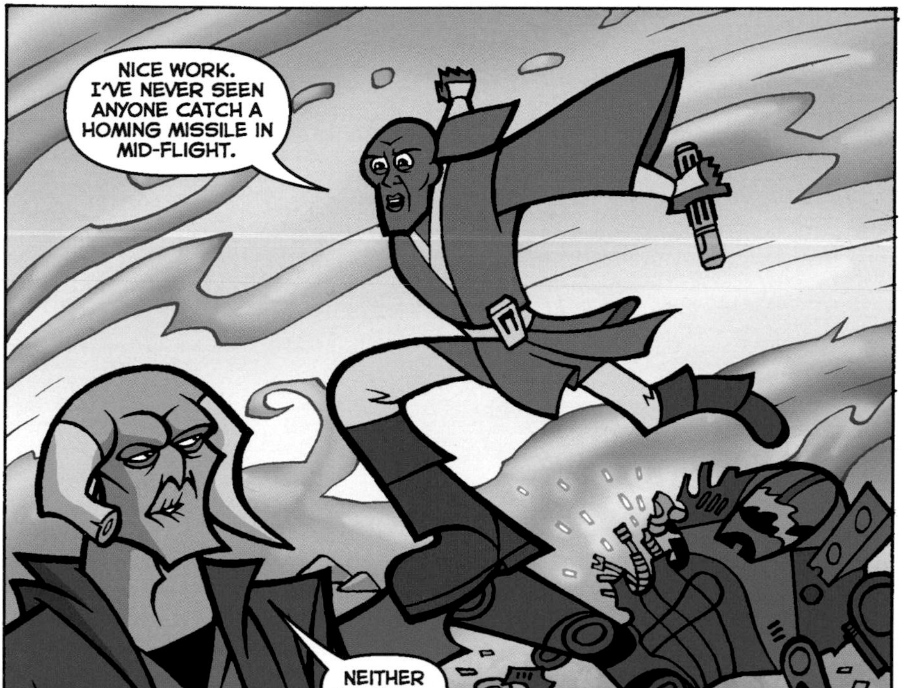
NICE WORK. I'VE NEVER SEEN ANYONE CATCH A HOMING MISSILE IN MID-FLIGHT.
NEITHER HAVE I...

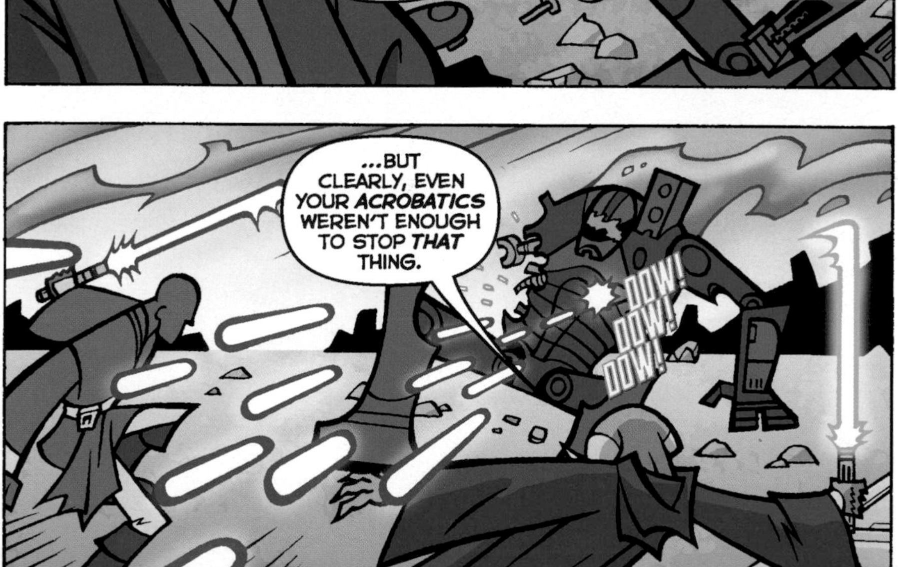
...BUT CLEARLY, EVEN YOUR *ACROBATICS* WEREN'T ENOUGH TO STOP *THAT* THING.
DOW! DOW! DOW!

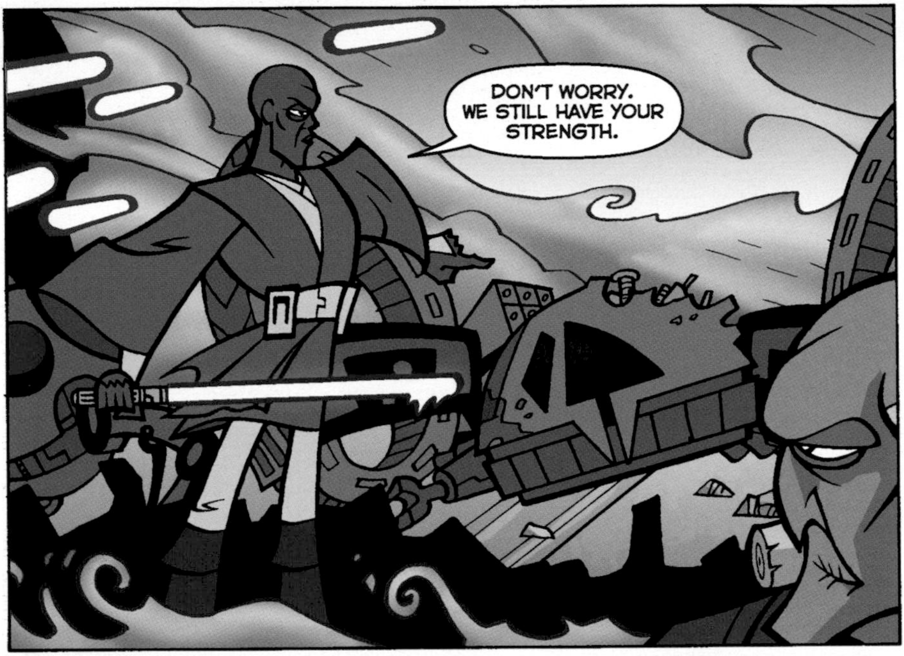
DON'T WORRY. WE STILL HAVE YOUR STRENGTH.

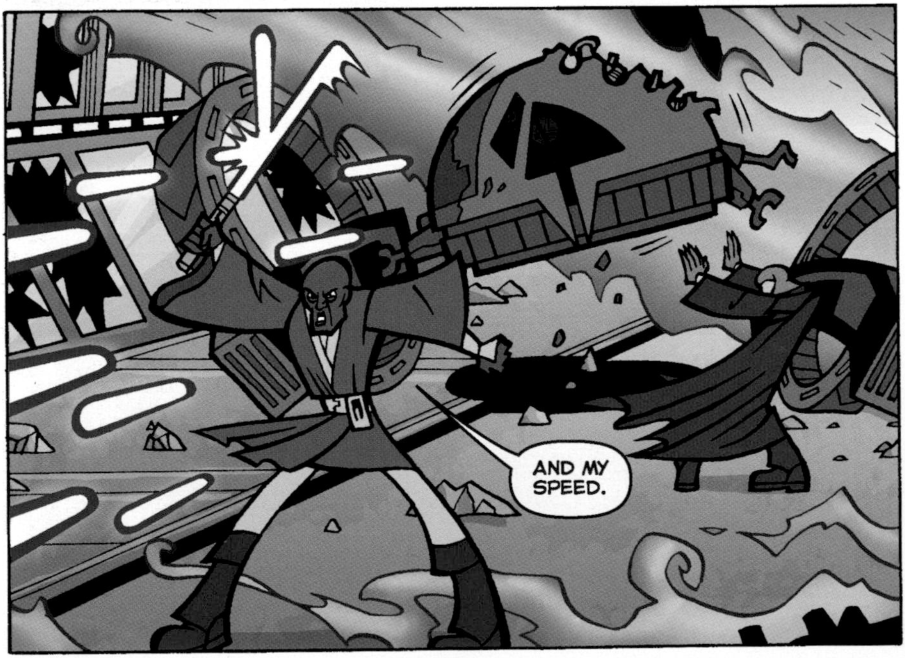
AND MY SPEED.

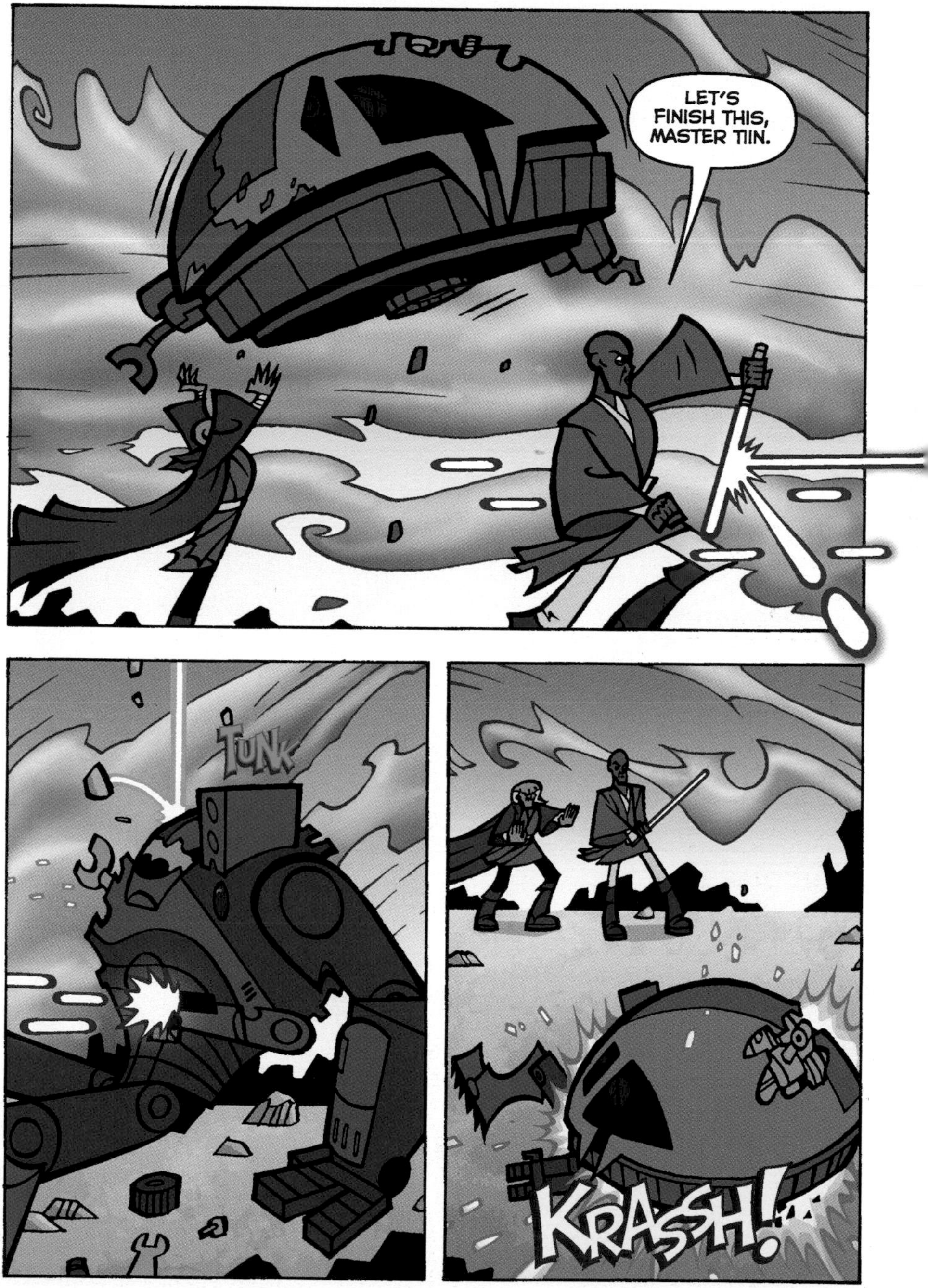
LET'S FINISH THIS, MASTER TIIN.
TUNK
KRASH!

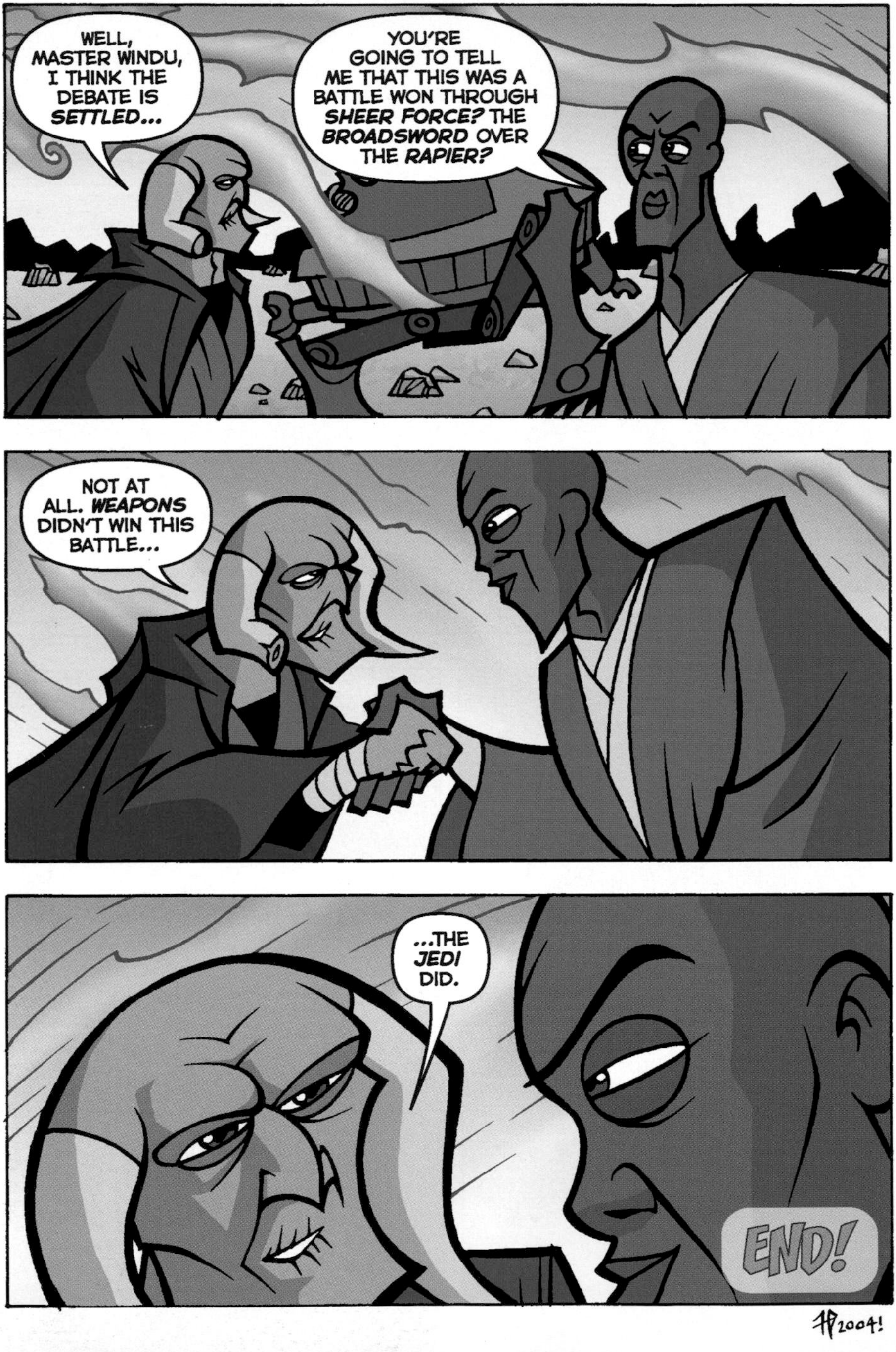
WELL, MASTER WINDU, I THINK THE DEBATE IS *SETTLED...*
YOU'RE GOING TO TELL ME THAT THIS WAS A BATTLE WON THROUGH *SHEER FORCE?* THE *BROADSWORD* OVER THE *RAPIER?*
NOT AT ALL. *WEAPONS* DIDN'T WIN THIS BATTLE...
...THE *JEDI* DID.
END!
2004!

STAR WARS
CLONE WARS
ADVENTURES

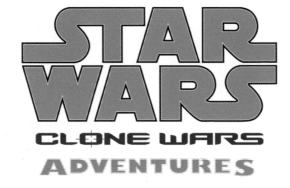

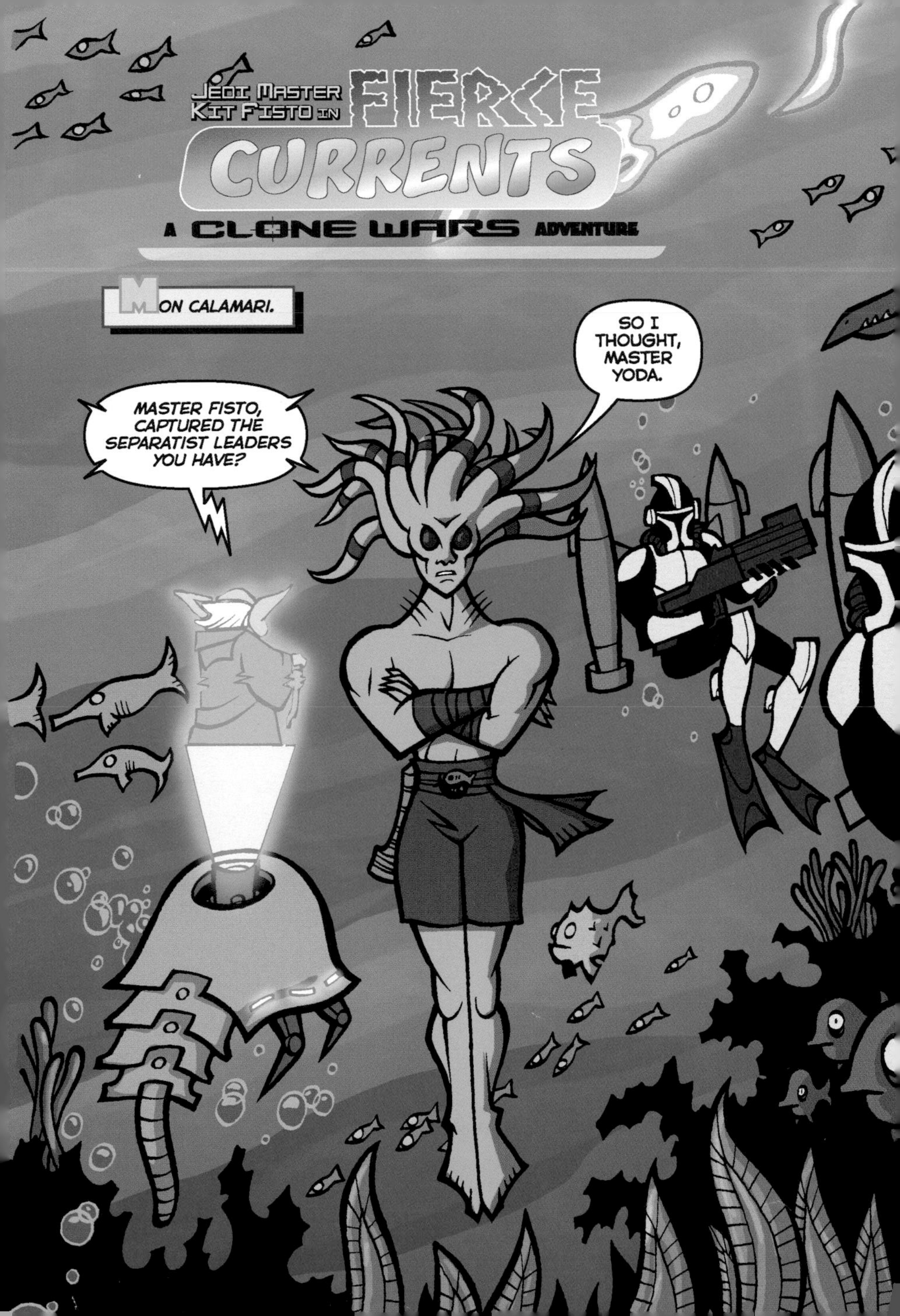
JEDI MASTER KIT FISTO IN
FIERCE CURRENTS
A CLONE WARS ADVENTURE
MON CALAMARI.
MASTER FISTO, CAPTURED THE SEPARATIST LEADERS YOU HAVE?
SO I THOUGHT, MASTER YODA.

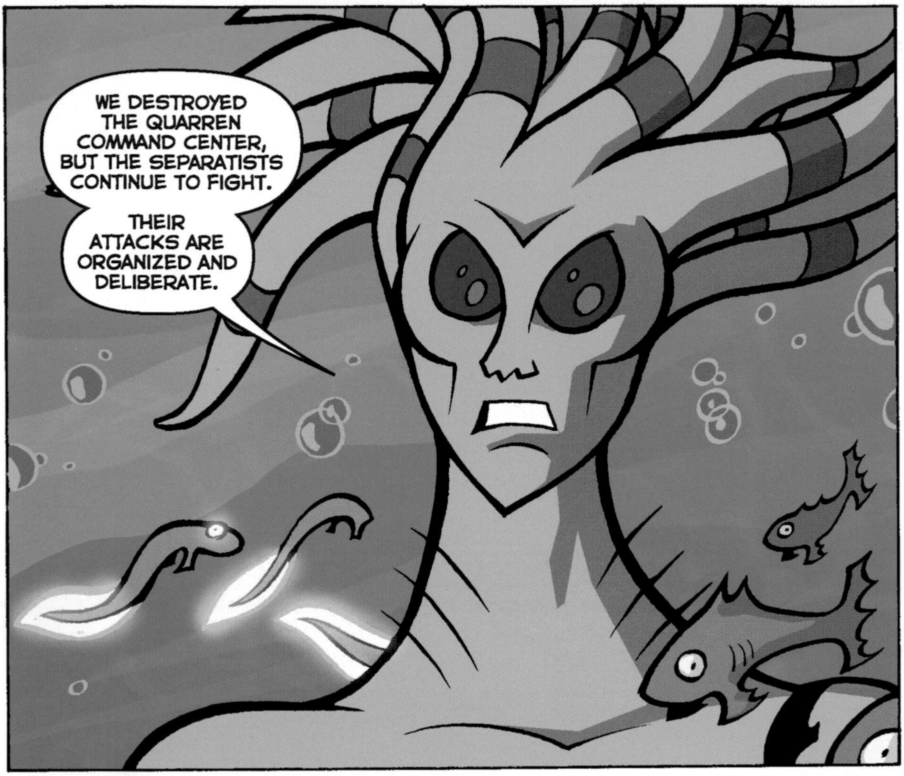
WE DESTROYED THE QUARREN COMMAND CENTER, BUT THE SEPARATISTS CONTINUE TO FIGHT.
THEIR ATTACKS ARE ORGANIZED AND DELIBERATE.

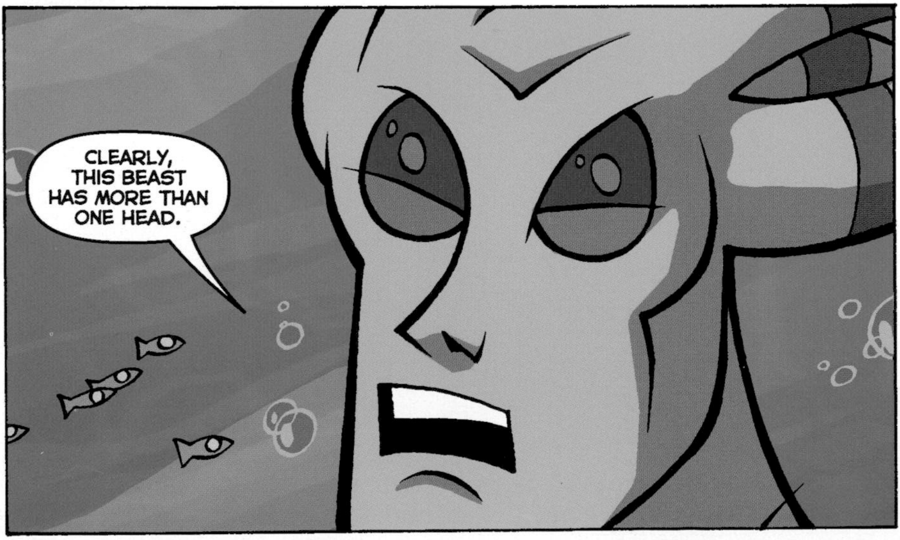
CLEARLY, THIS BEAST HAS MORE THAN ONE HEAD.

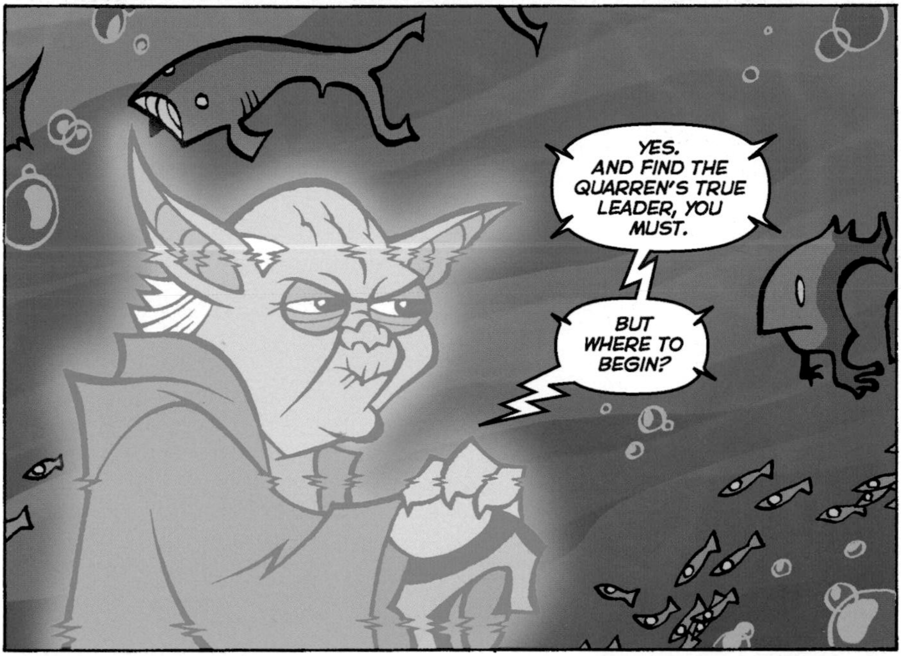
YES. AND FIND THE QUARREN'S TRUE LEADER, YOU MUST.
BUT WHERE TO BEGIN?

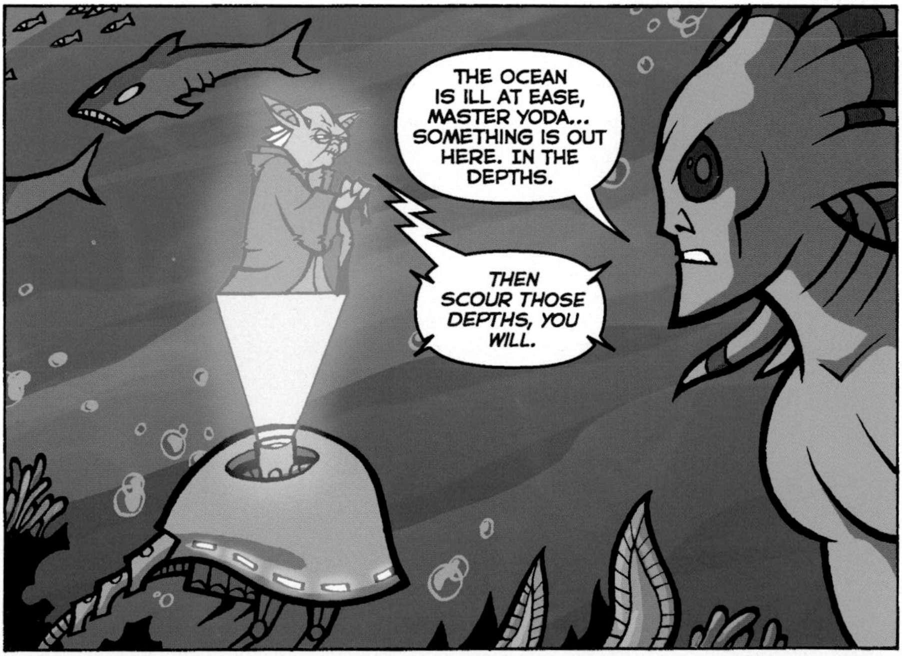
THE OCEAN IS ILL AT EASE, MASTER YODA... SOMETHING IS OUT HERE. IN THE DEPTHS.
THEN SCOUR THOSE DEPTHS, YOU WILL.

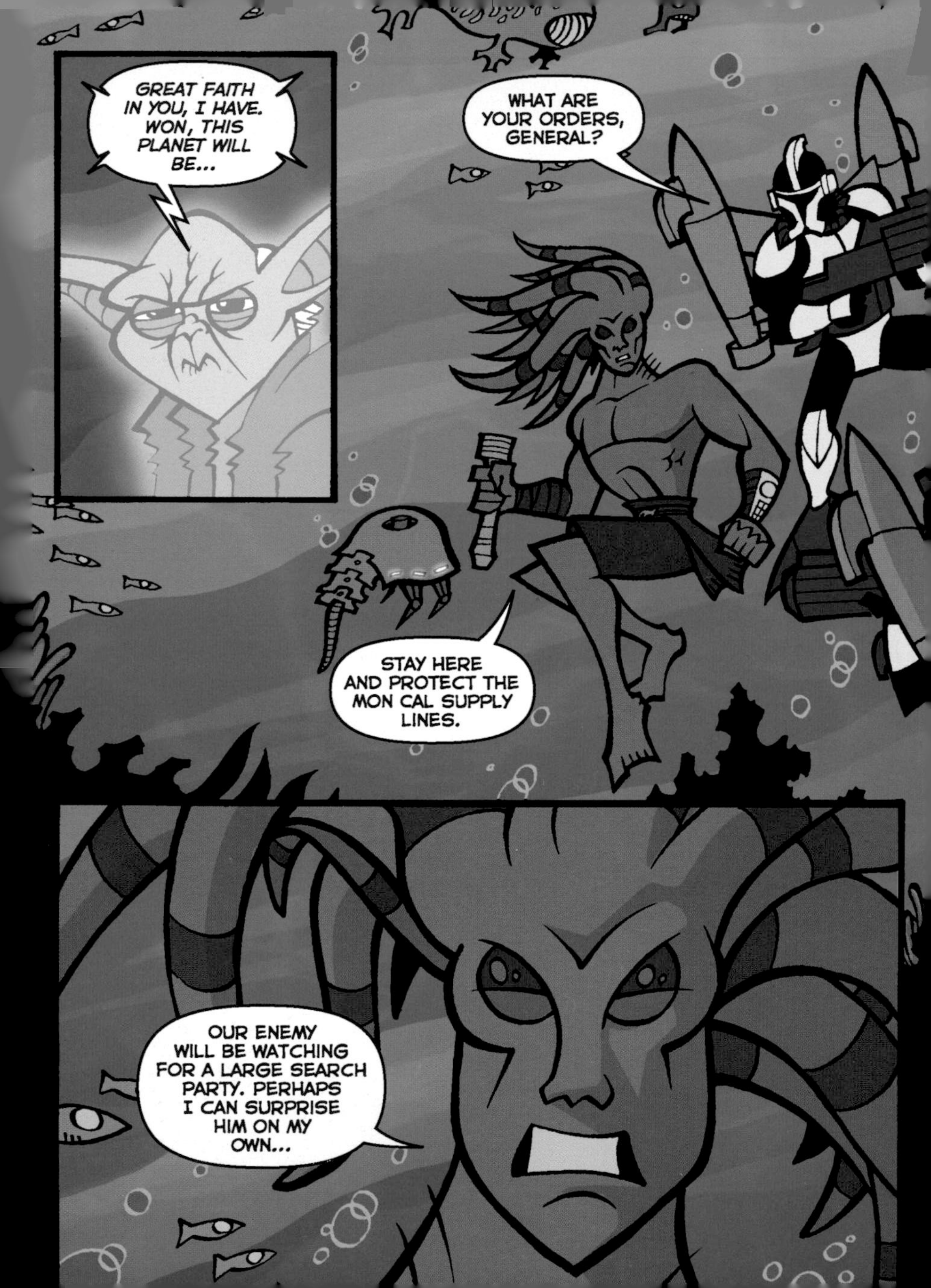
GREAT FAITH IN YOU, I HAVE. WON, THIS PLANET WILL BE...
WHAT ARE YOUR ORDERS, GENERAL?
STAY HERE AND PROTECT THE MON CAL SUPPLY LINES.
OUR ENEMY WILL BE WATCHING FOR A LARGE SEARCH PARTY. PERHAPS I CAN SURPRISE HIM ON MY OWN...

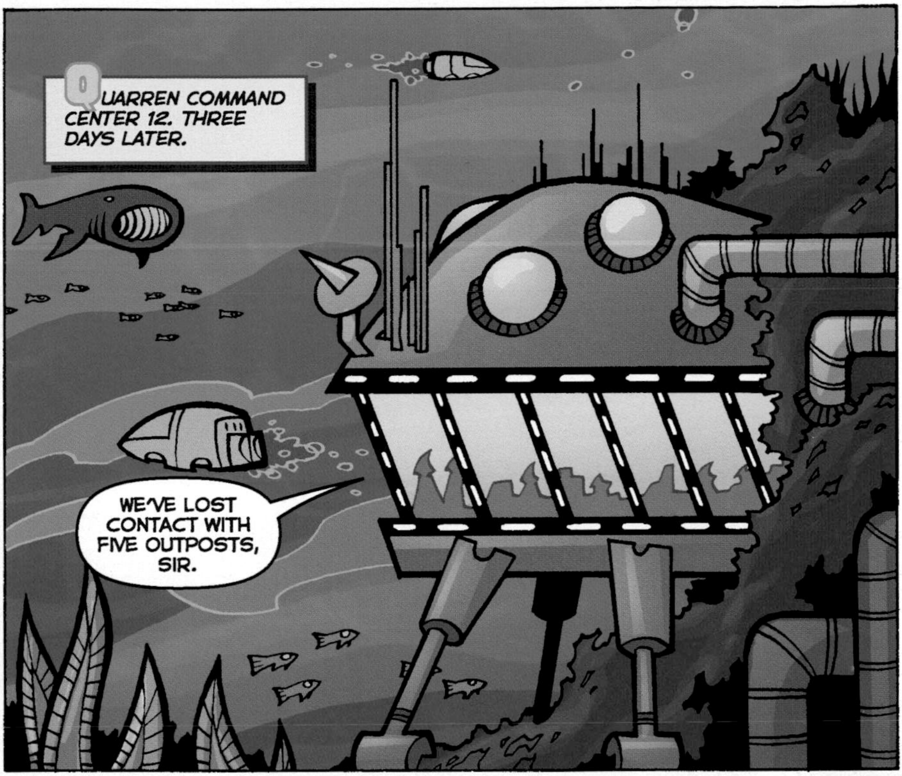
QUARREN COMMAND CENTER 12. THREE DAYS LATER.
WE'VE LOST CONTACT WITH FIVE OUTPOSTS, SIR.

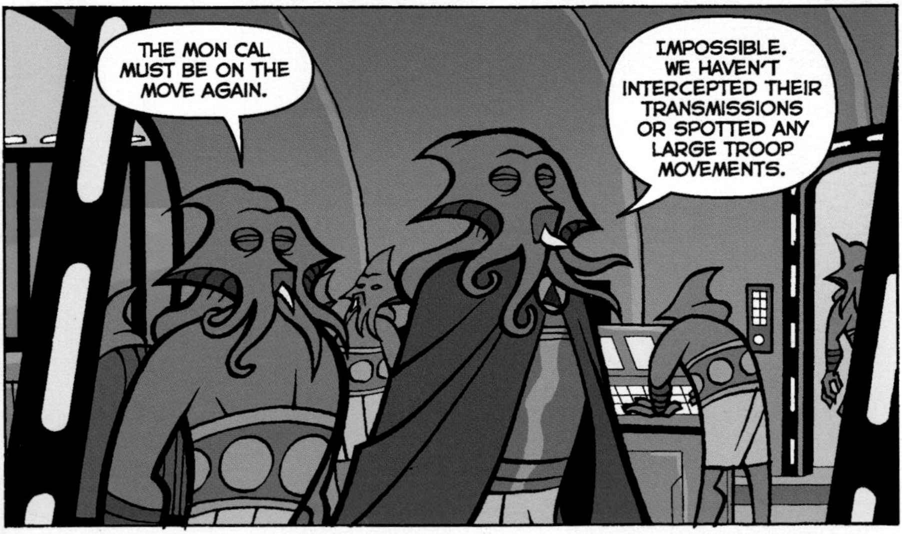
THE MON CAL MUST BE ON THE MOVE AGAIN.
IMPOSSIBLE. WE HAVEN'T INTERCEPTED THEIR TRANSMISSIONS OR SPOTTED ANY LARGE TROOP MOVEMENTS.

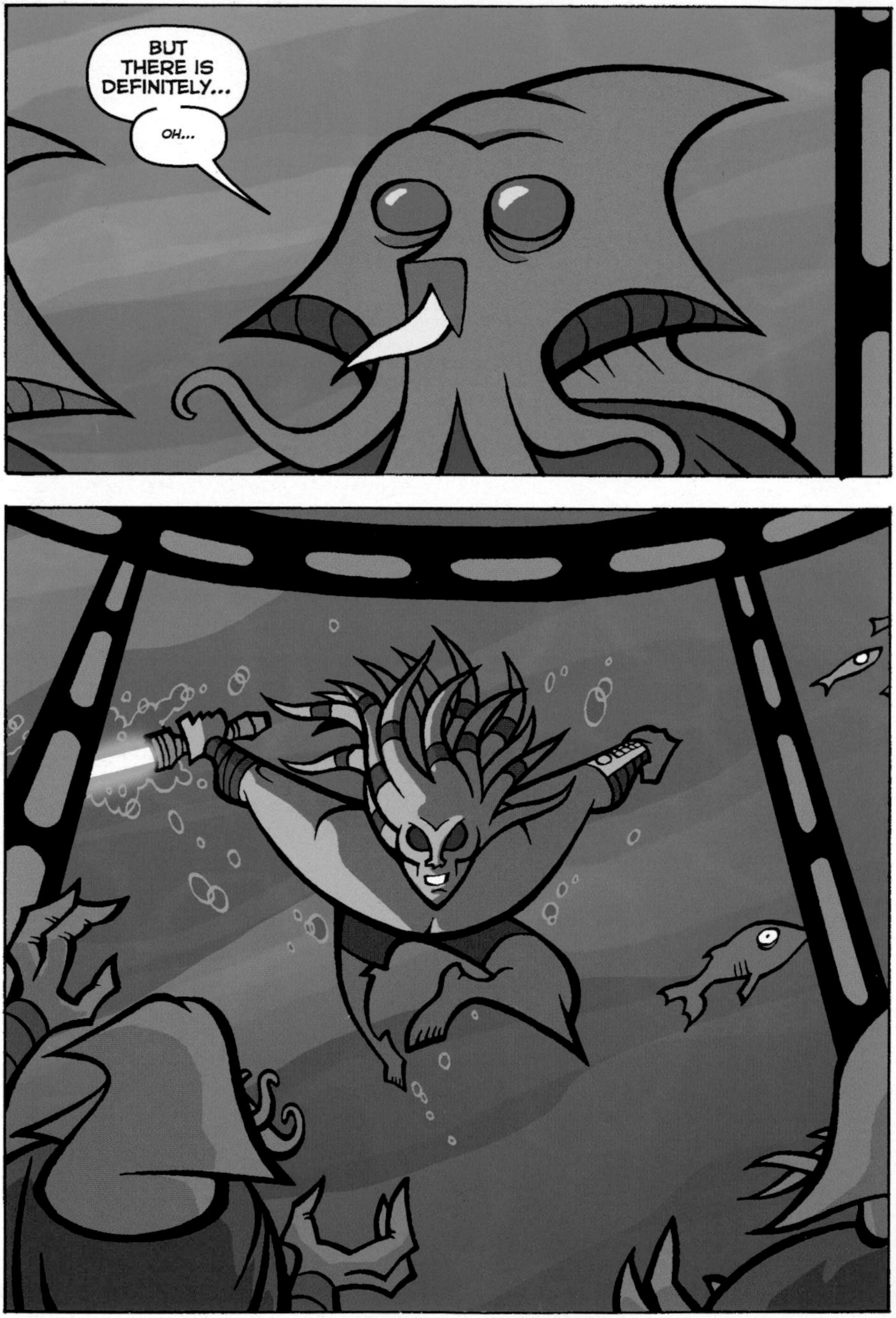
BUT THERE IS DEFINITELY...
OH...

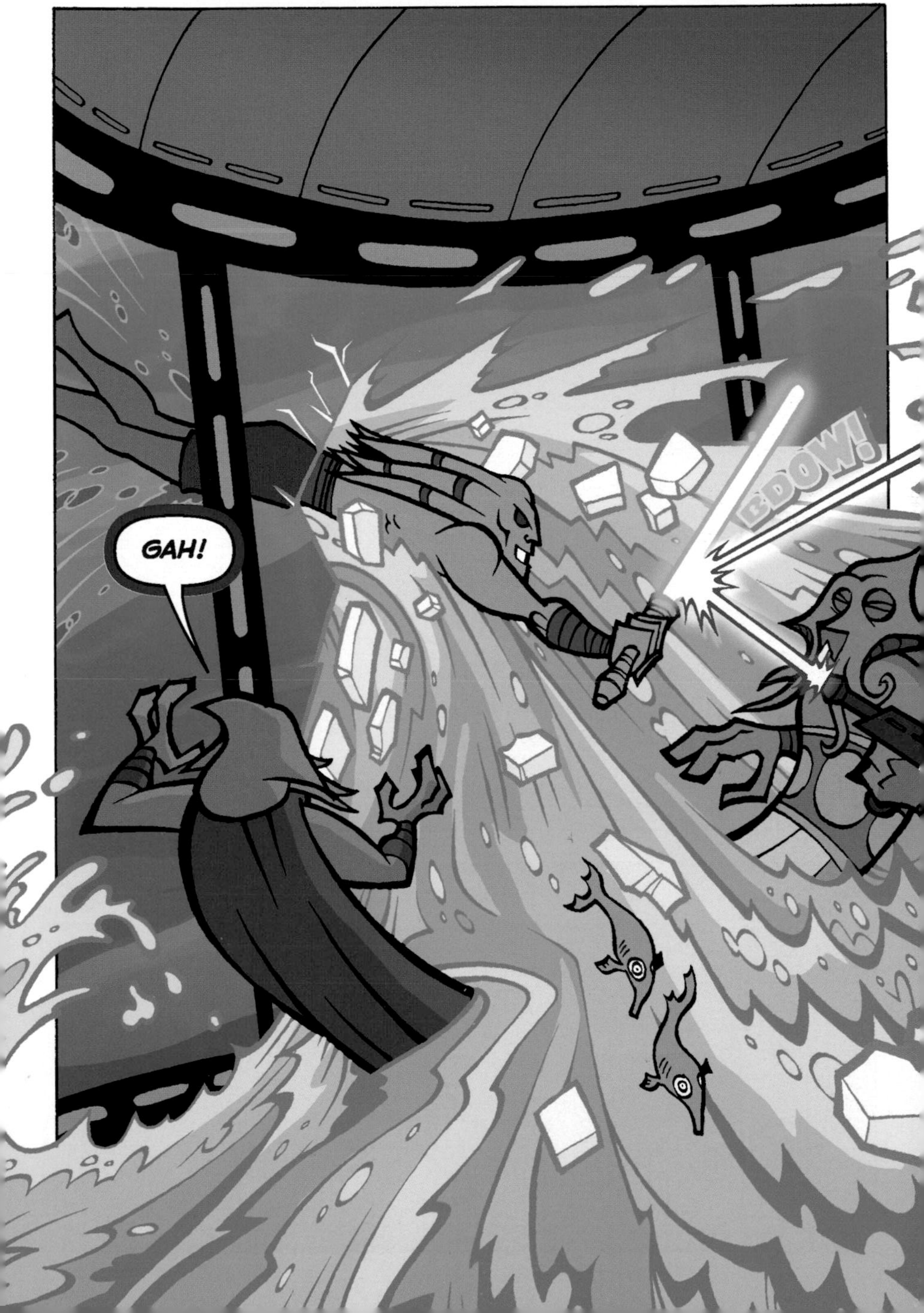
GAH!
BDOW!

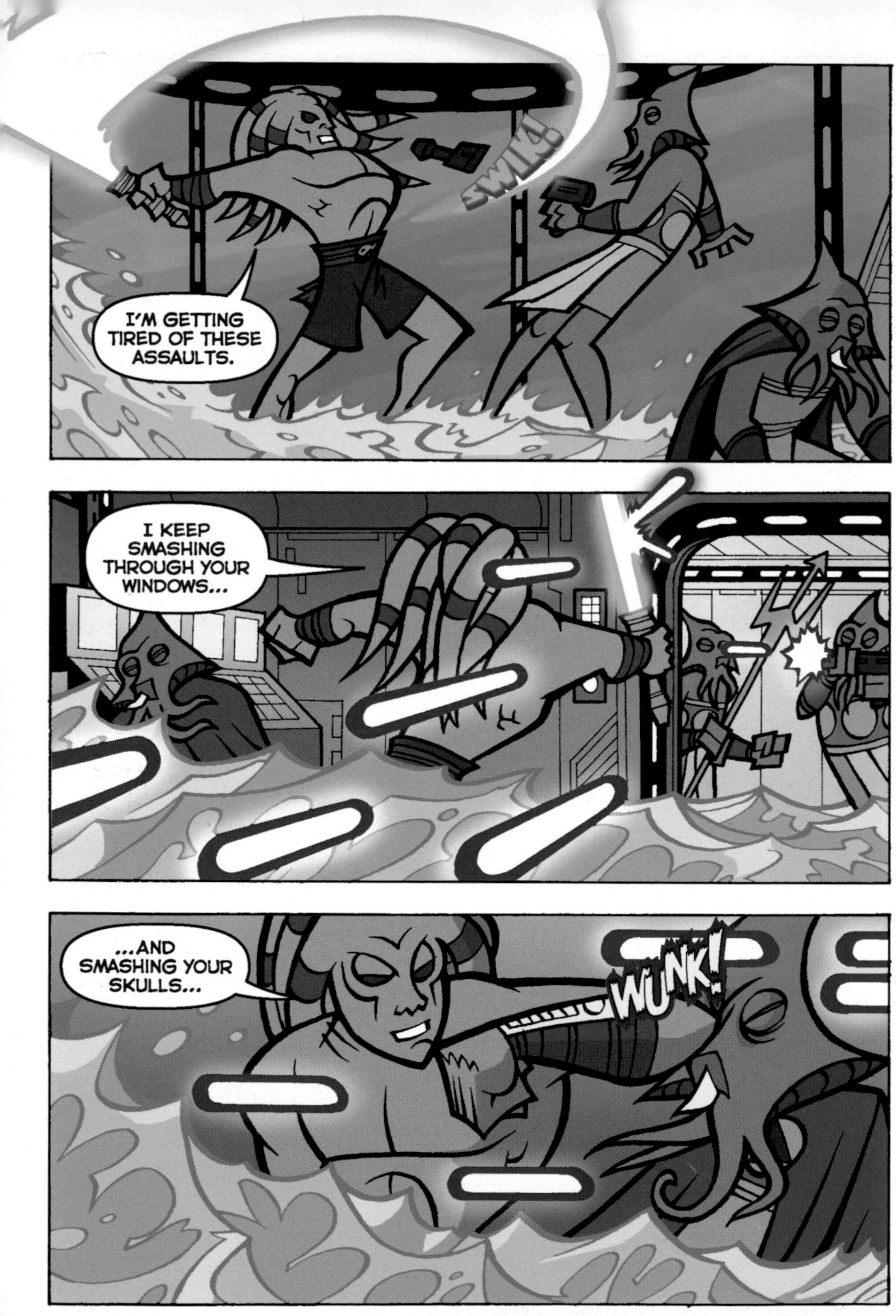
SWIK!
I'M GETTING TIRED OF THESE ASSAULTS.
I KEEP SMASHING THROUGH YOUR WINDOWS...
...AND SMASHING YOUR SKULLS...
WUNK!

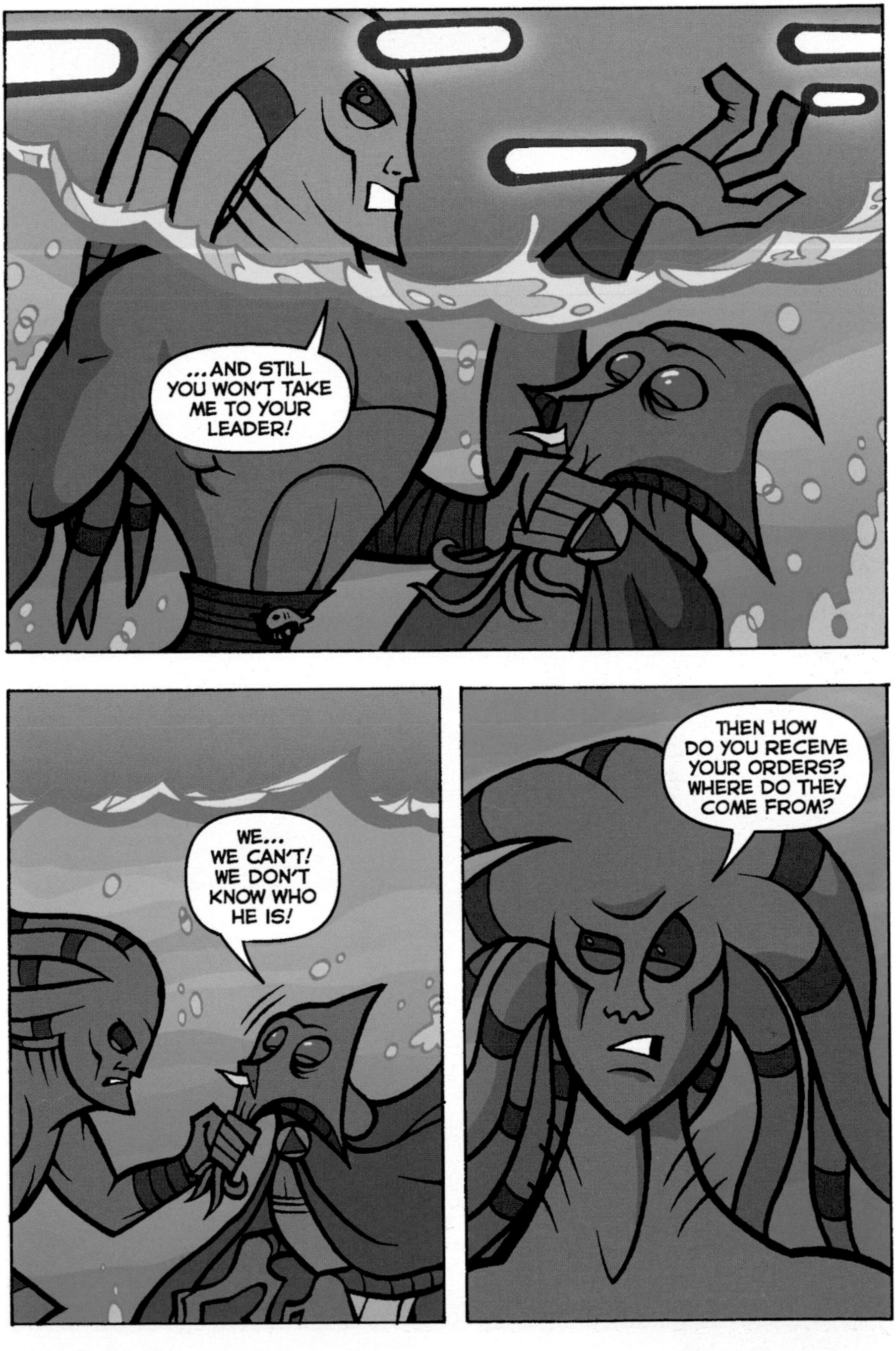
...AND STILL YOU WON'T TAKE ME TO YOUR LEADER!
WE... WE CAN'T! WE DON'T KNOW WHO HE IS!
THEN HOW DO YOU RECEIVE YOUR ORDERS? WHERE DO THEY COME FROM?

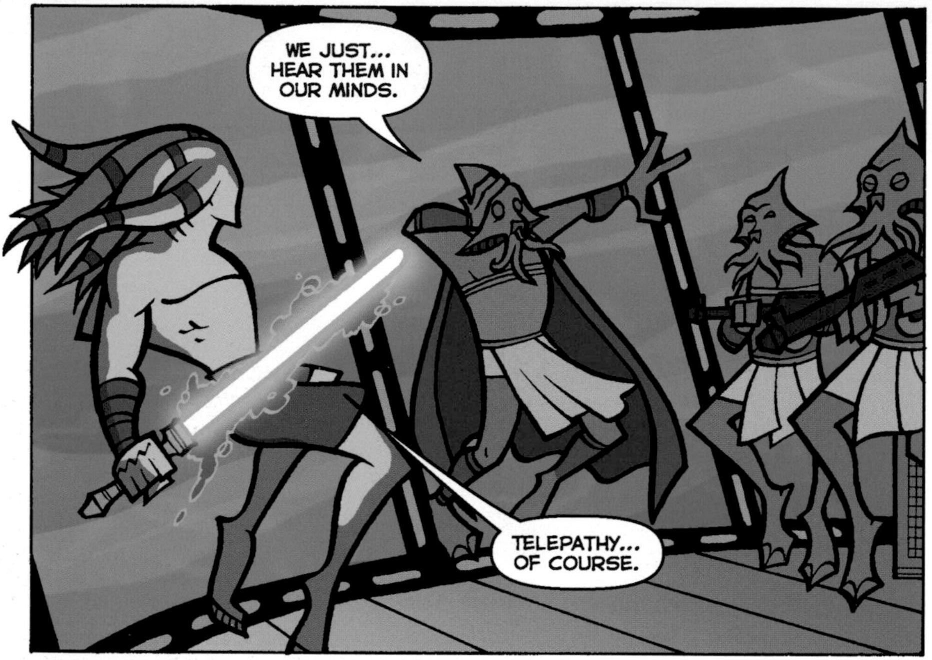
WE JUST... HEAR THEM IN OUR MINDS.
TELEPATHY... OF COURSE.

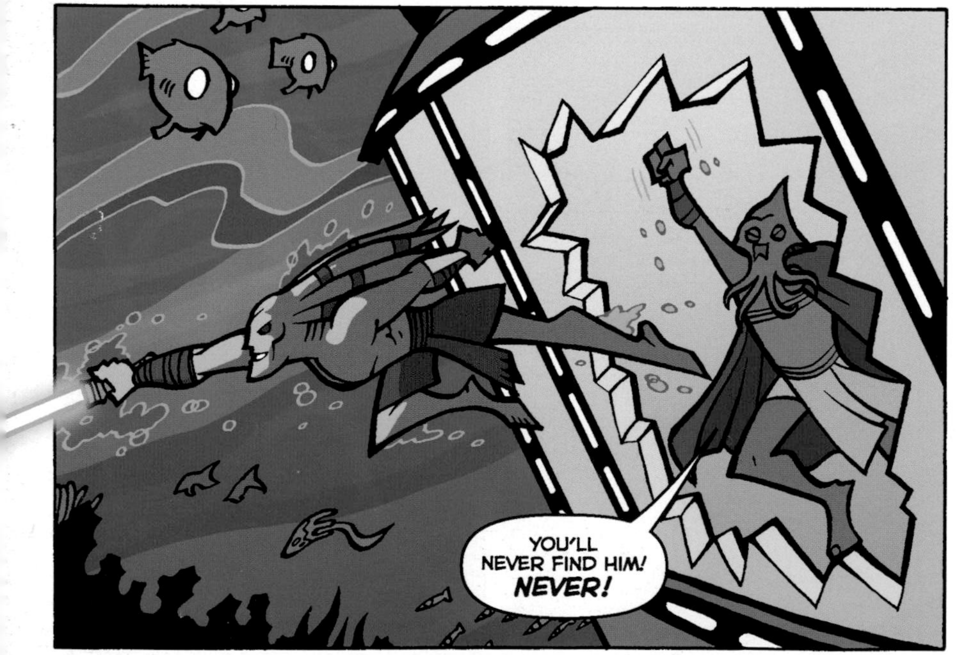
YOU'LL NEVER FIND HIM! ***NEVER!***

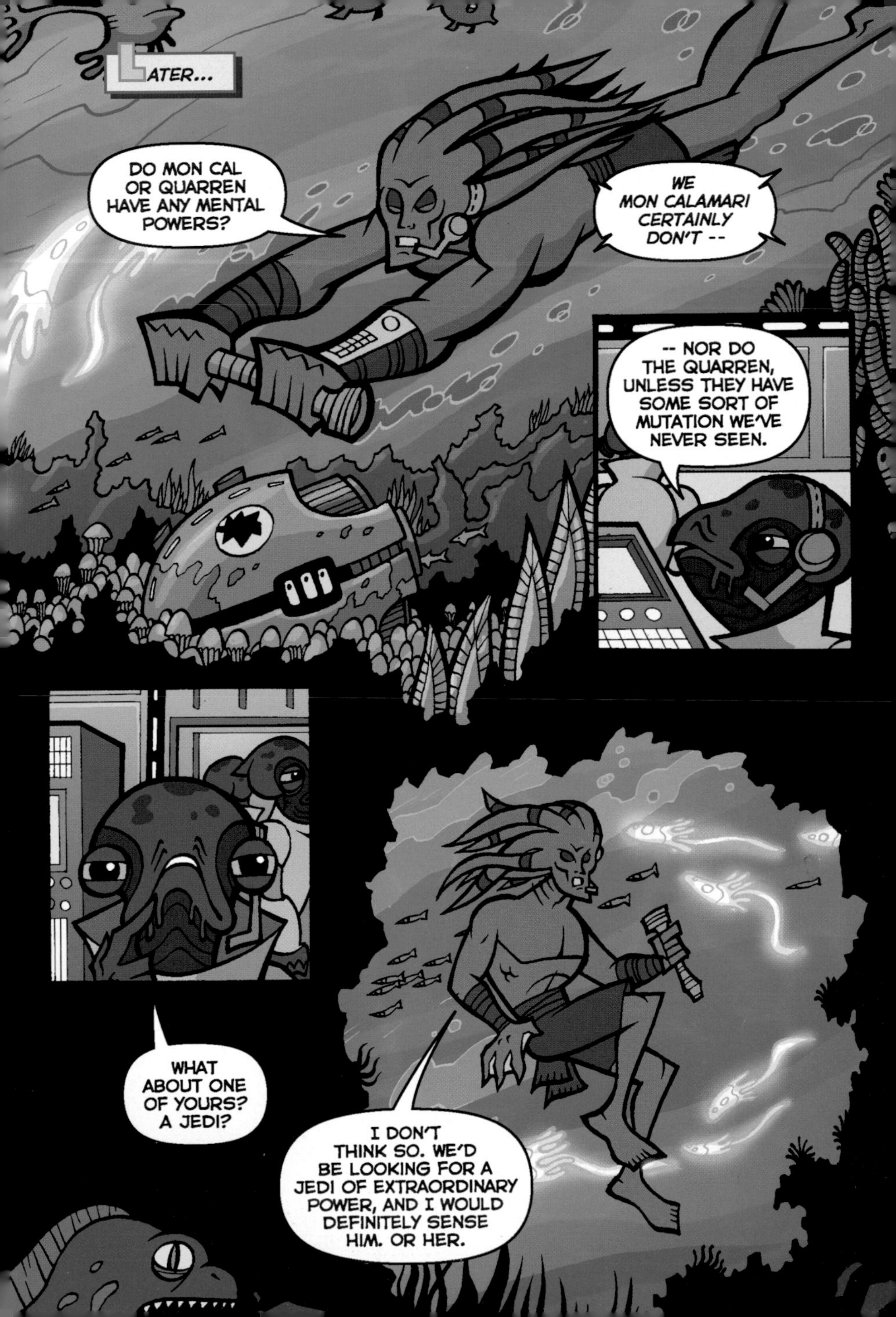
LATER...
DO MON CAL OR QUARREN HAVE ANY MENTAL POWERS?
WE MON CALAMARI CERTAINLY DON'T --
-- NOR DO THE QUARREN, UNLESS THEY HAVE SOME SORT OF MUTATION WE'VE NEVER SEEN.
WHAT ABOUT ONE OF YOURS? A JEDI?
I DON'T THINK SO. WE'D BE LOOKING FOR A JEDI OF EXTRAORDINARY POWER, AND I WOULD DEFINITELY SENSE HIM. OR HER.

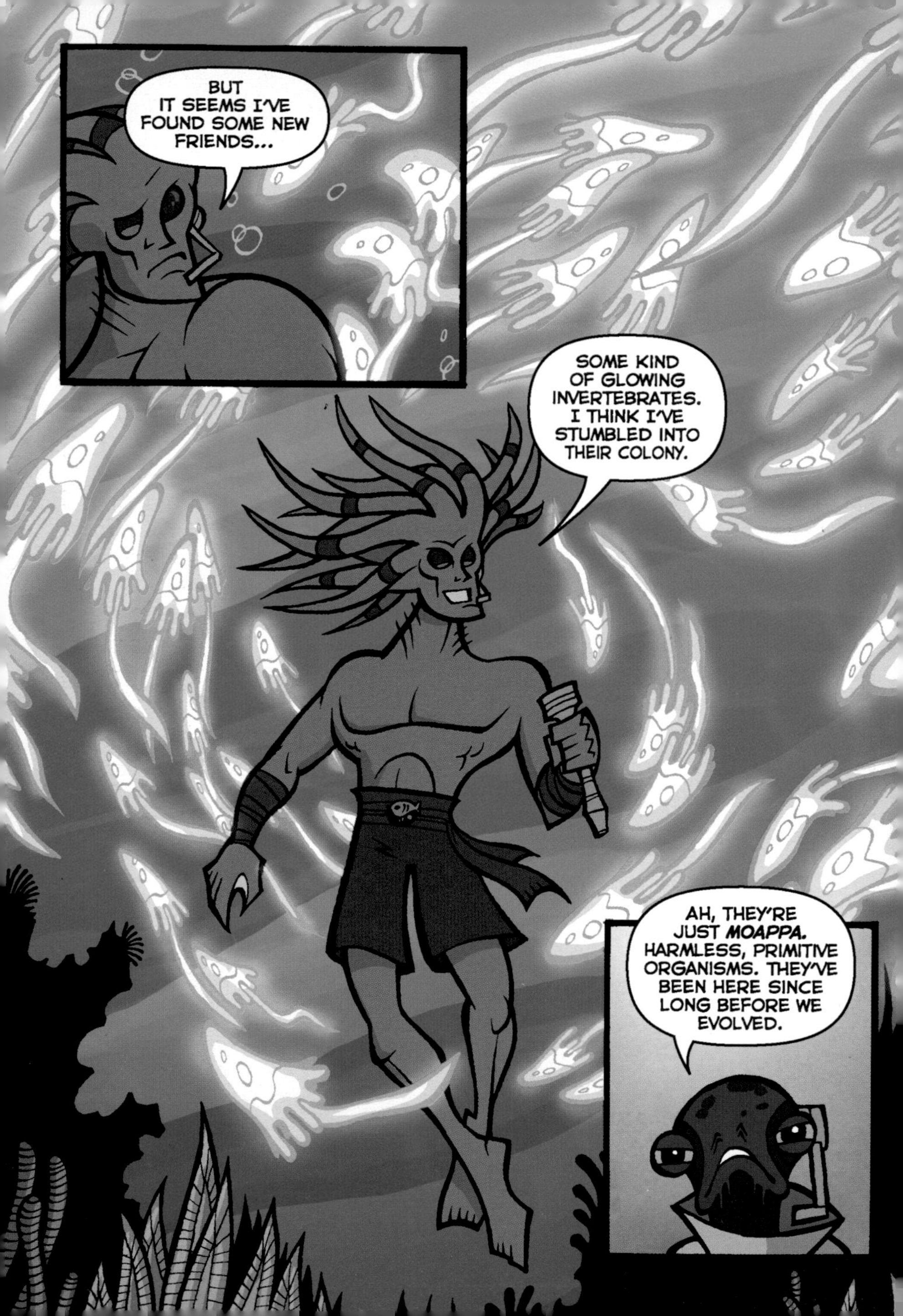
BUT IT SEEMS I'VE FOUND SOME NEW FRIENDS...
SOME KIND OF GLOWING INVERTEBRATES. I THINK I'VE STUMBLED INTO THEIR COLONY.
AH, THEY'RE JUST ***MOAPPA.*** HARMLESS, PRIMITIVE ORGANISMS. THEY'VE BEEN HERE SINCE LONG BEFORE WE EVOLVED.

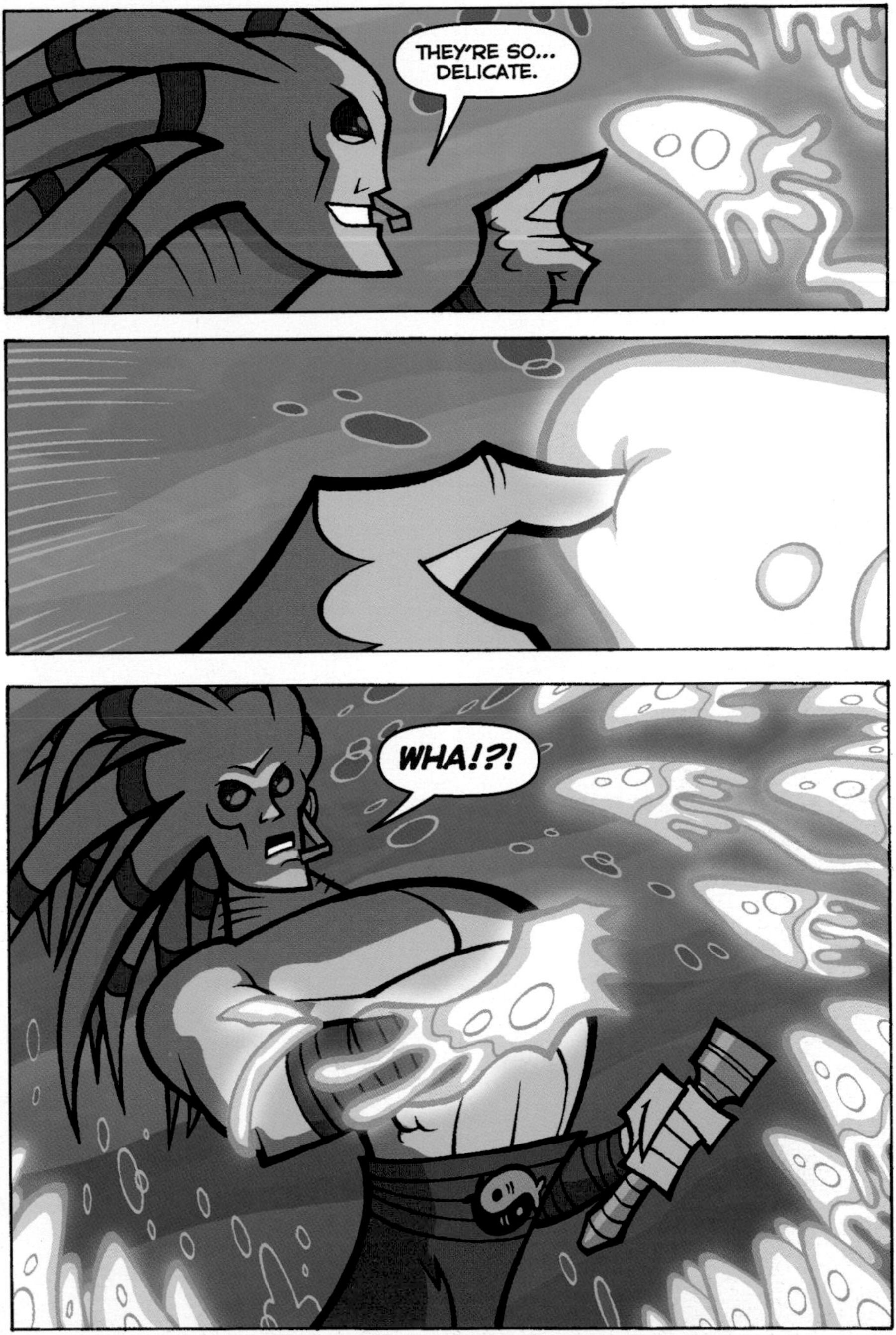
THEY'RE SO...
DELICATE.
WHA!?!

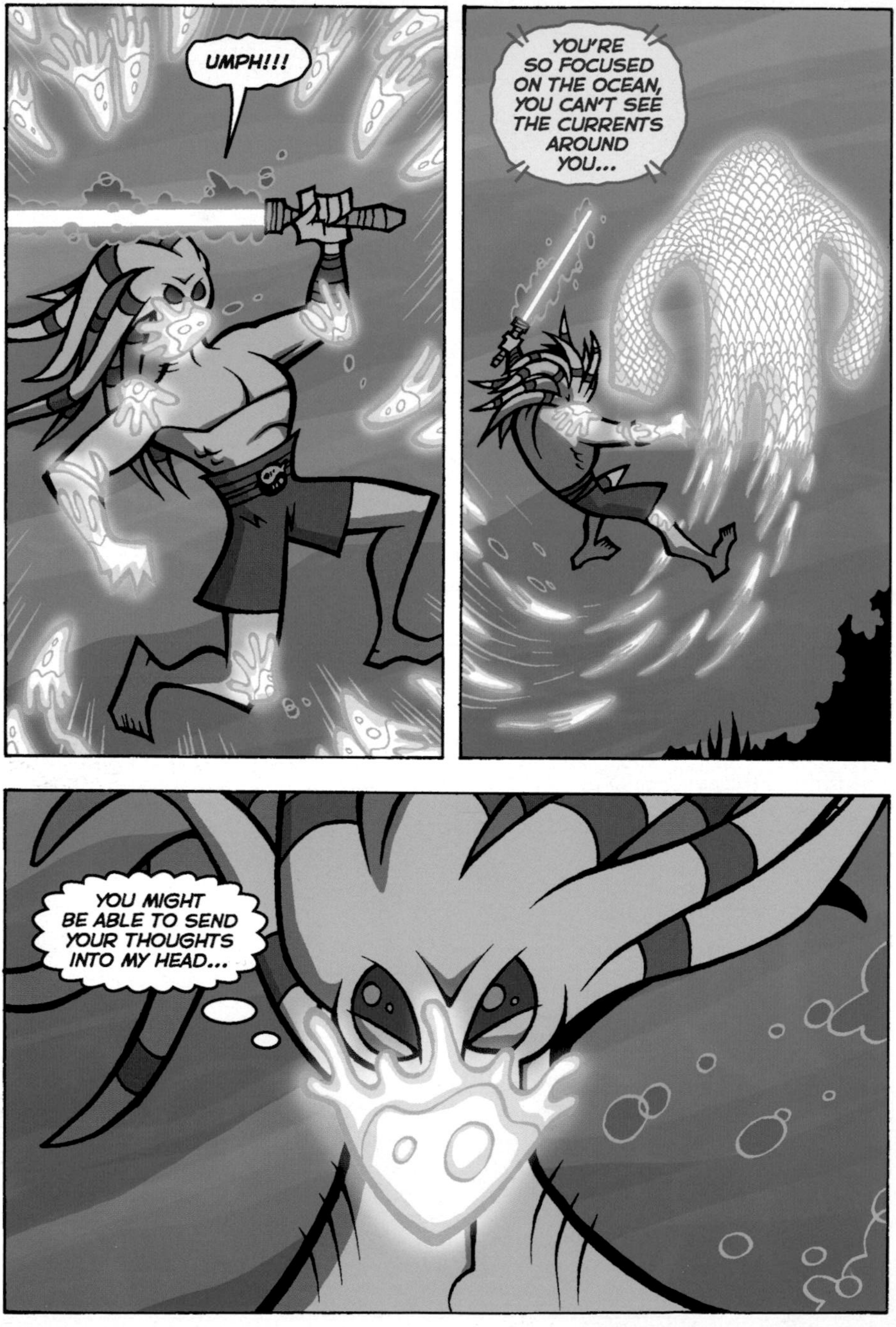
UMPH!!!
YOU'RE SO FOCUSED ON THE OCEAN, YOU CAN'T SEE THE CURRENTS AROUND YOU...
YOU MIGHT BE ABLE TO SEND YOUR THOUGHTS INTO MY HEAD...

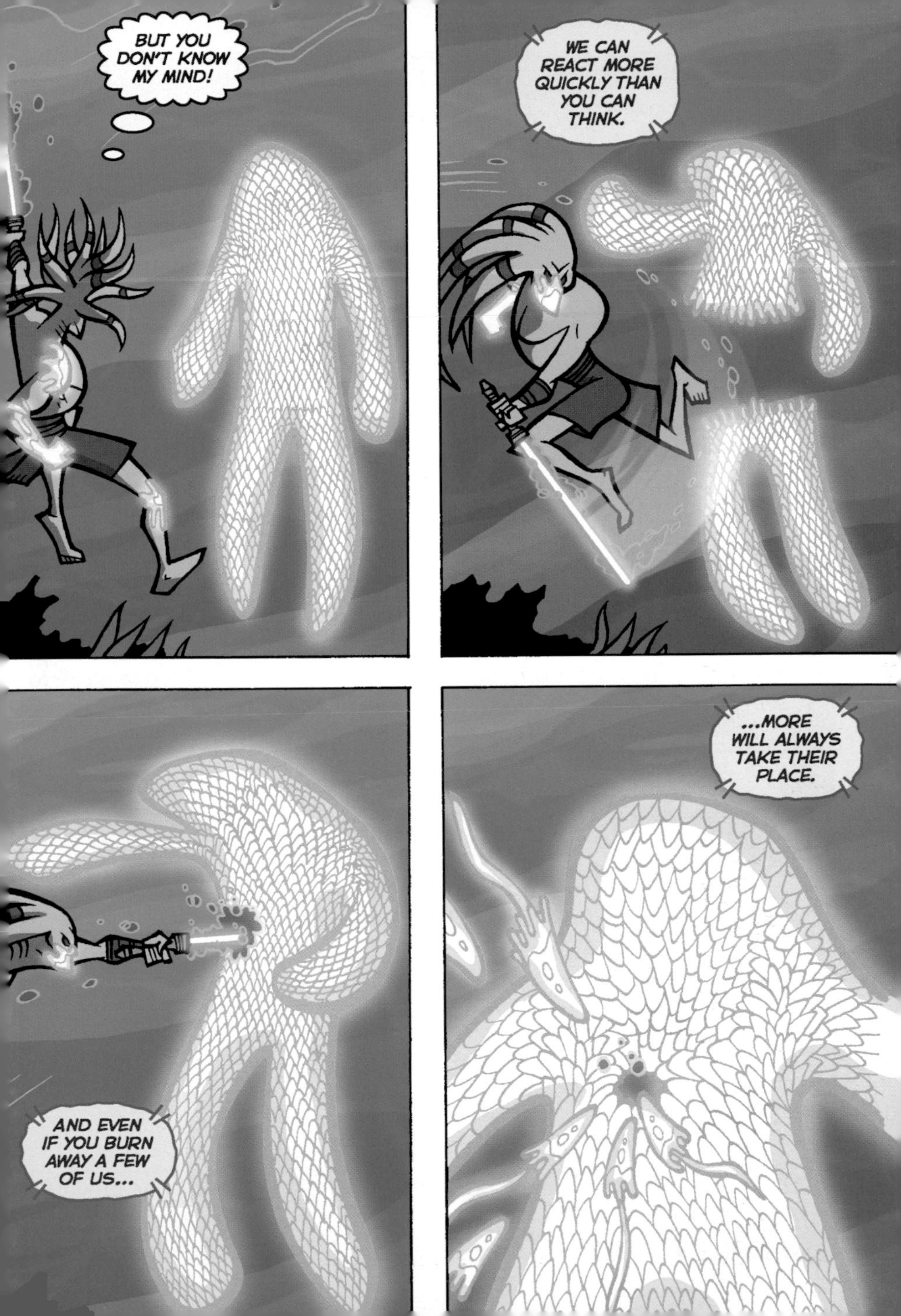
BUT YOU DON'T KNOW MY MIND!
WE CAN REACT MORE QUICKLY THAN YOU CAN THINK.
AND EVEN IF YOU BURN AWAY A FEW OF US...
...MORE WILL ALWAYS TAKE THEIR PLACE.

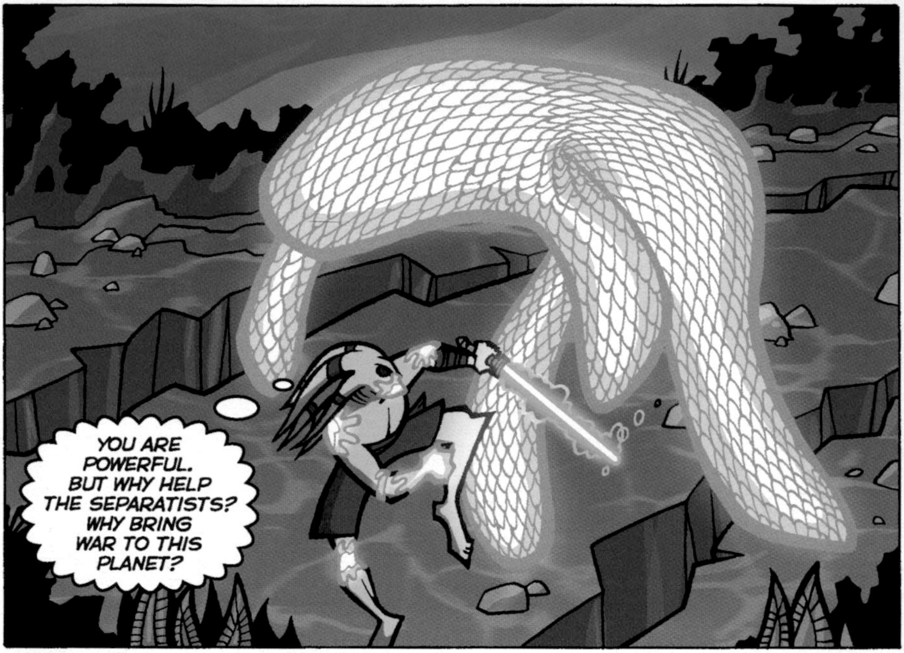
YOU ARE POWERFUL. BUT WHY HELP THE SEPARATISTS? WHY BRING WAR TO THIS PLANET?

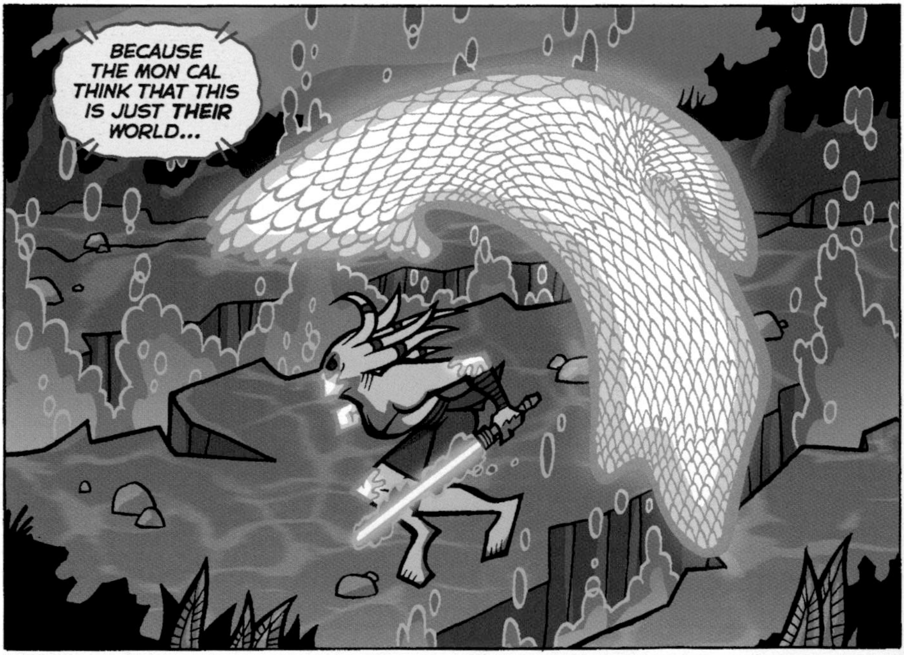
BECAUSE THE MON CAL THINK THAT THIS IS JUST THEIR WORLD...

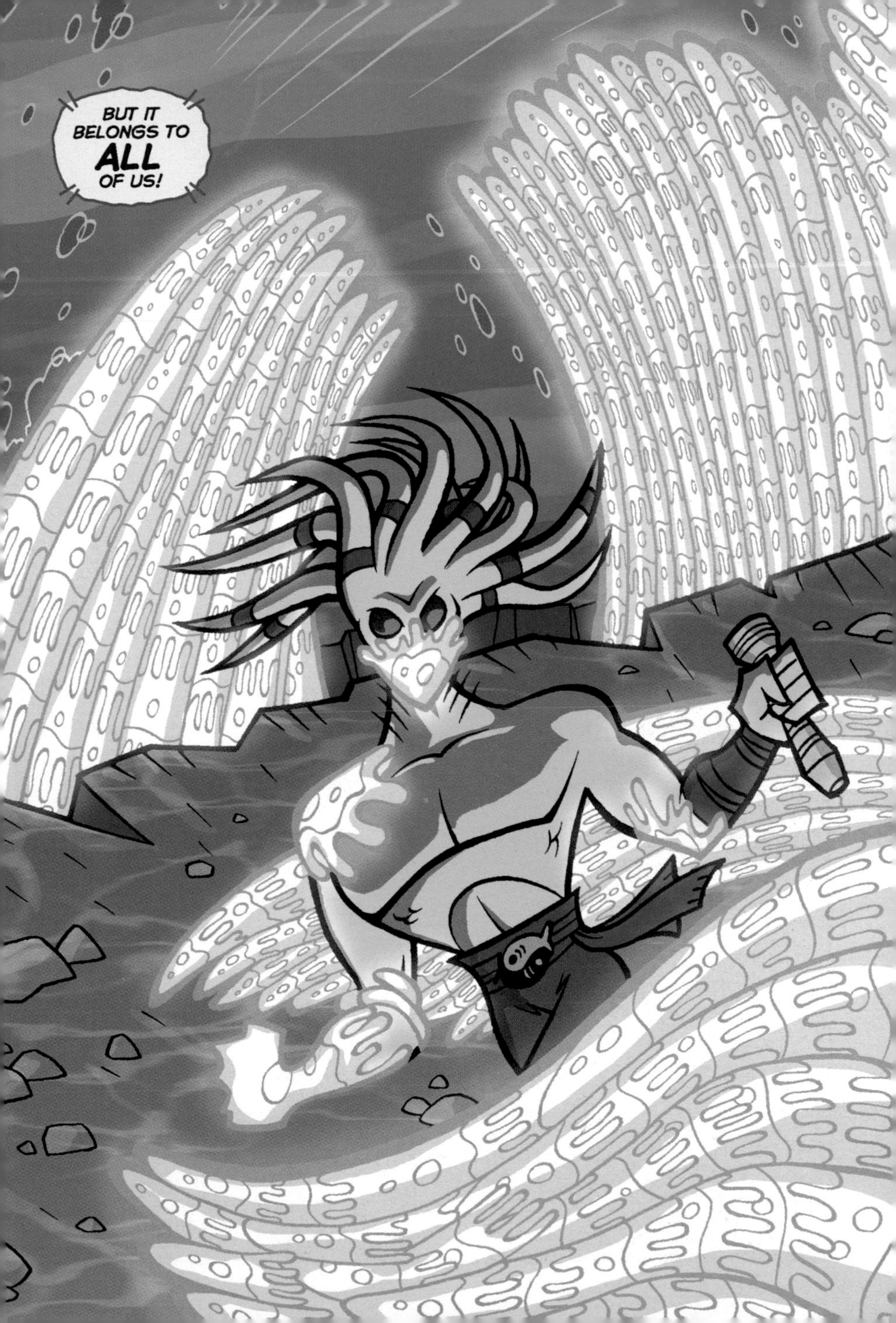
BUT IT BELONGS TO ALL OF US!

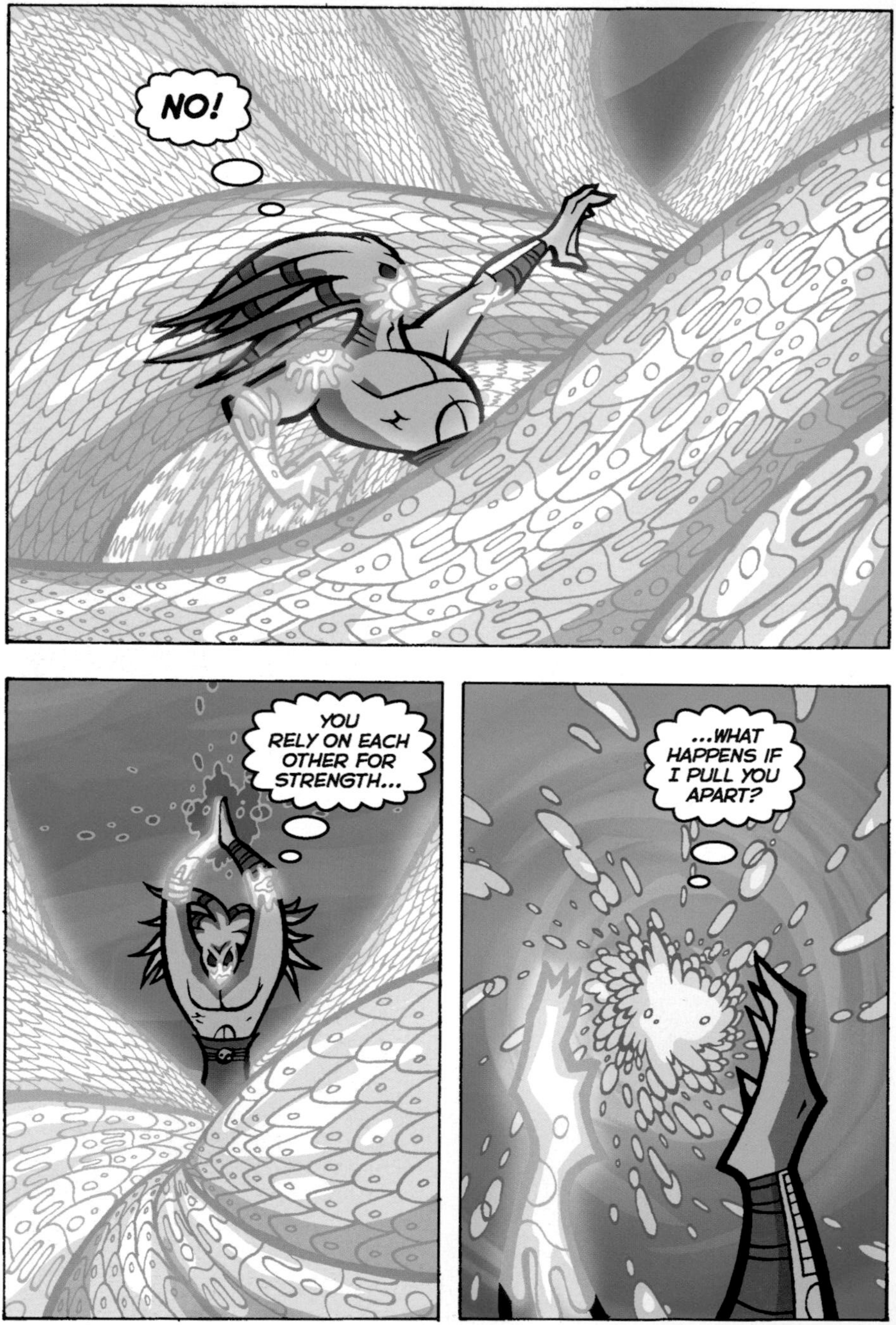
NO!
YOU RELY ON EACH OTHER FOR STRENGTH...
...WHAT HAPPENS IF I PULL YOU APART?

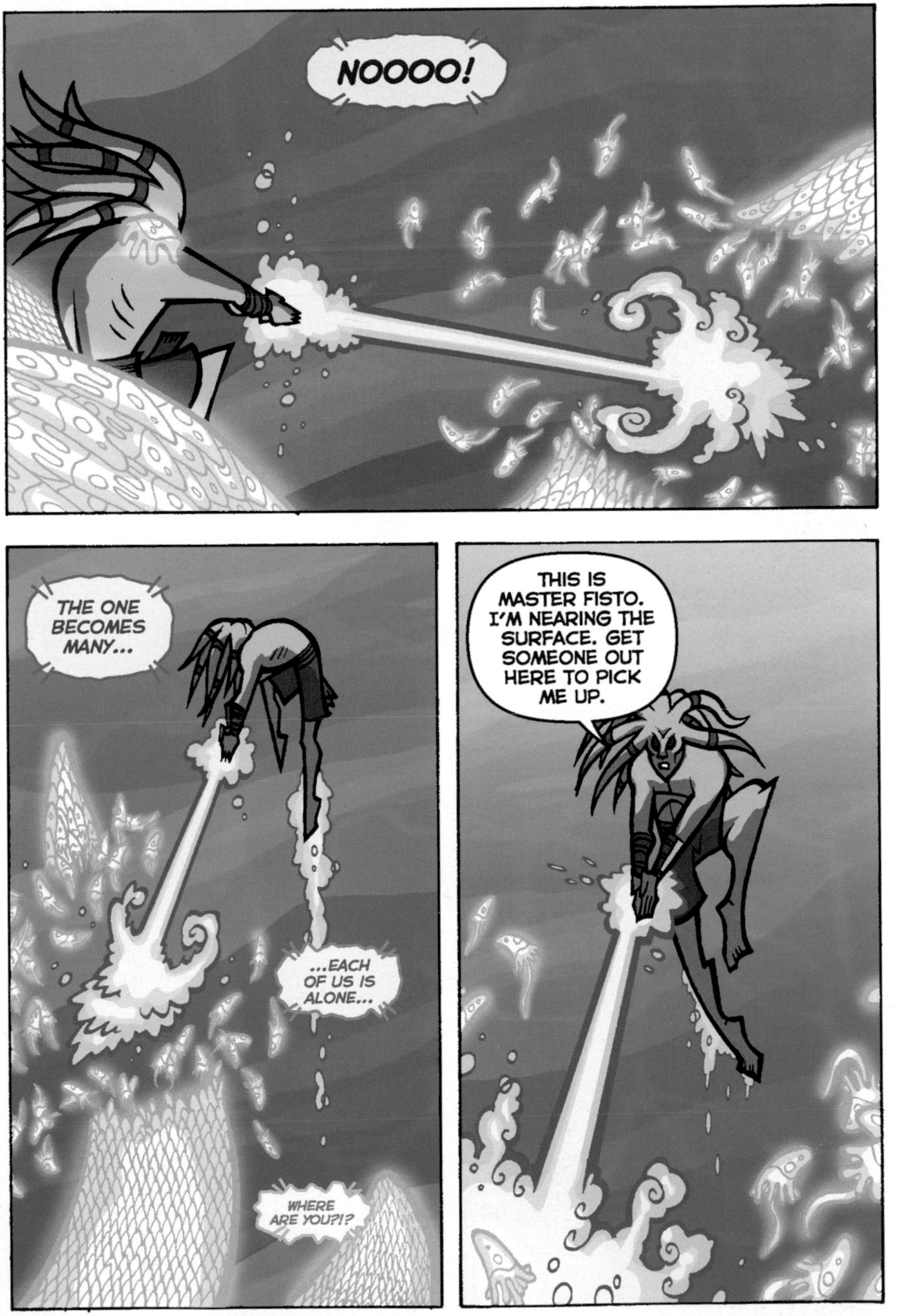
NOOOO!
THE ONE BECOMES MANY...
...EACH OF US IS ALONE...
WHERE ARE YOU?!?
THIS IS MASTER FISTO. I'M NEARING THE SURFACE. GET SOMEONE OUT HERE TO PICK ME UP.

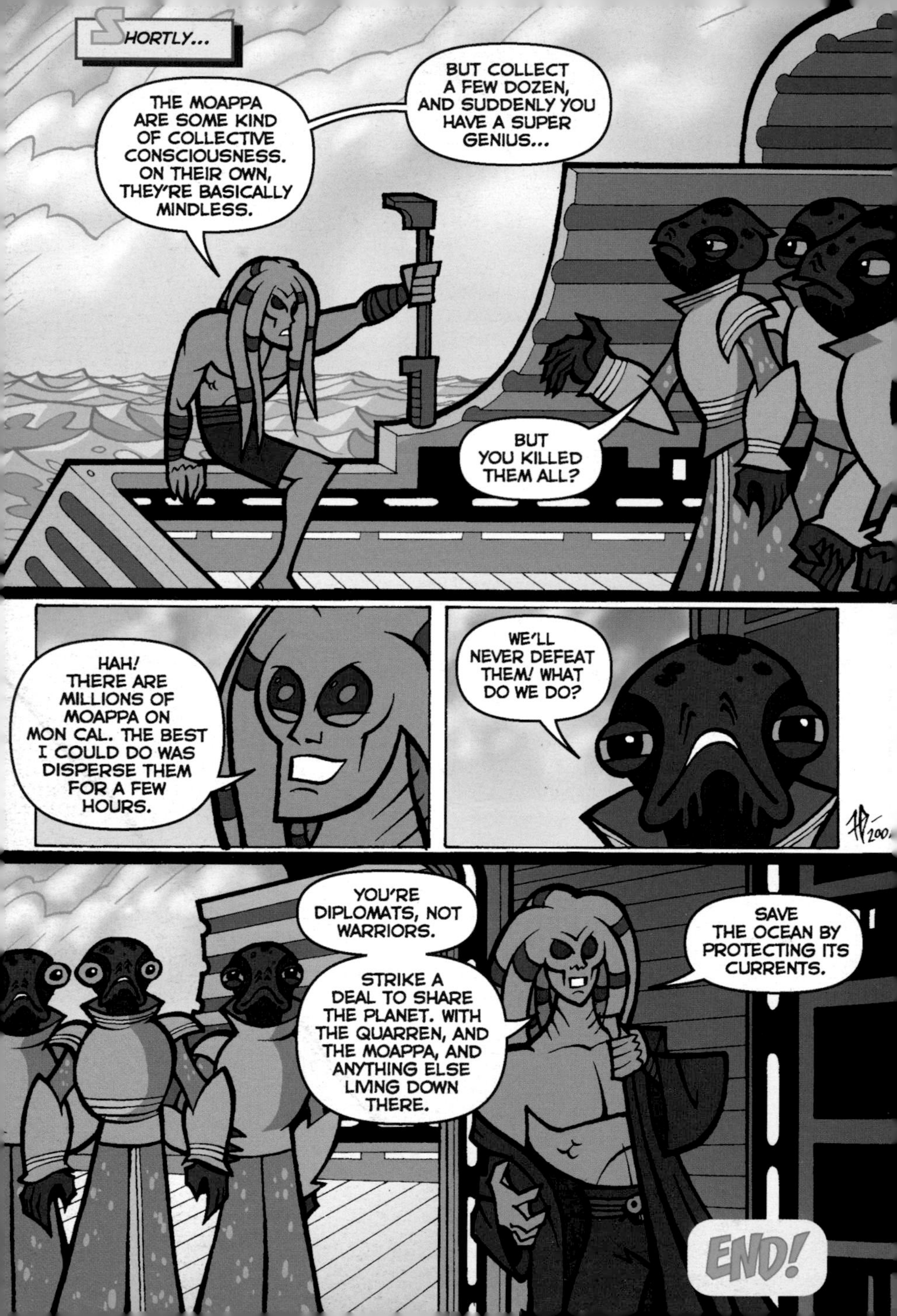
SHORTLY...
THE MOAPPA ARE SOME KIND OF COLLECTIVE CONSCIOUSNESS. ON THEIR OWN, THEY'RE BASICALLY MINDLESS.
BUT COLLECT A FEW DOZEN, AND SUDDENLY YOU HAVE A SUPER GENIUS...
BUT YOU KILLED THEM ALL?
HAH! THERE ARE MILLIONS OF MOAPPA ON MON CAL. THE BEST I COULD DO WAS DISPERSE THEM FOR A FEW HOURS.
WE'LL NEVER DEFEAT THEM! WHAT DO WE DO?
YOU'RE DIPLOMATS, NOT WARRIORS.
STRIKE A DEAL TO SHARE THE PLANET. WITH THE QUARREN, AND THE MOAPPA, AND ANYTHING ELSE LIVING DOWN THERE.
SAVE THE OCEAN BY PROTECTING ITS CURRENTS.
END!

STAR WARS™

GRAPHIC NOVELS FROM TITAN BOOKS

	MOVIE STAR WARS EPISODE I PHANTOM MENACE 32 BSW4	MOVIE STAR WARS EPISODE II ATTACK OF THE CLONES 22 BSW4	MOVIE STAR WARS EPISODE III 19 BSW 4

SITH ERA

PREQUEL I, II, III

SITH ERA		PREQUEL I, II, III	
Star Wars: Tales of the Jedi – The Collection (feat. Knights of the Old Republic) 4000 BSW4	Star Wars: Episode I Phantom Menace 32 BSW4	Star Wars: Episode II Attack of the Clones 22 BSW4	Star Wars: Boba Fett – Enemy of the Empire 3 BSW4
Star Wars: Tales of the Jedi – The Sith War 3998 BSW4	Star Wars: Episode I Adventures 32 BSW4	Star Wars: Episode II Villains Pack (Jango Fett, Zam Wesell) 22 BSW4	Star Wars: Underworld – The Yavin Vassilika 1 BSW4
Star Wars: Tales of the Jedi – Redemption 3996 BSW4	Star Wars: Outlander 32 BSW4		
Star Wars: Jedi Vs. Sith 1000 BSW4	Star Wars: Emissaries to Malastare 32 BSW4	Star Wars: The Clone Wars – The Defense of Kamino 22 BSW4	
52 BSW4 Star Wars: Jango Fett – Open Seasons	Star Wars: Darkness 31 BSW4	Star Wars: The Clone Wars Victories & Sacrifices 22 BSW4	
Star Wars: Jedi Council – Acts of War 33 BSW4	Star Wars: Twilight 31 BSW4		
Star Wars: Prelude to Rebellion 33 BSW4	Star Wars: The Hunt for Aurra Sing 30 BSW4		
Star Wars: Darth Maul 33 BSW4			
Star Wars: Bounty Hunters 32 ASW4			

STAR WARS™

◀▶ GRAPHIC NOVELS FROM TITAN BOOKS

MOVIE STAR WARS EPISODE IV A NEW HOPE 0 SW4	**MOVIE STAR WARS EPISODE V THE EMPIRE STRIKES BACK 3 ASW4**	**MOVIE STAR WARS EPISODE VI RETURN OF THE JEDI 4 ASW4**

OUTSIDE STAR WARS CONTINUITY

Star Wars: Infinities – A New Hope
INFINITIES

Star Wars: Infinities – The Empire Strikes Back INFINITIES

TALES FROM ACROSS THE STAR WARS UNIVERSE

YEAR 0

Star Wars: Vader's Quest
0 ASW4

Star Wars: Empire 1 0-5 ASW4

Star Wars : Empire 2 0-5 ASW4

Star Wars: Splinter of the Mind's Eye
2 ASW4

Star Wars: Shadows of the Empire - Evolution 4 ASW4

Star Wars: X-Wing Rogue Squadron- In the Empire's Service 4 ASW4

Star Wars: X-Wing Rogue Squadron – Masquerade 4 ASW4

Star Wars: X-Wing Rogue Squadron – The Warrior Princess 4 ASW4

Star Wars: X-Wing Rogue Squadron – Blood & Honour 4 ASW4

Star Wars: X-Wing Rogue Squadron – Mandatory Retirement 4 ASW4

Star Wars: X-Wing Rogue Squadron – Requiem for a Rogue 4 ASW4

THE NEW REPUBLIC

Star Wars: The Last Command
5 ASW4

Star Wars: Heir to the Empire
9 ASW4

Star Wars: Dark Empire (New Edition)
10 ASW4

Star Wars: Union
20 ASW4

Star Wars — A Long Time Ago... Doomworld (Vol. 1)
SPAN MULTIPLE ERAS

Star Wars – A Long Time Ago... Dark Encounters (Vol.2)
SPAN MULTIPLE ERAS

Star Wars – A Long Time Ago... Resurrection of Evil (Vol 3)
SPAN MULTIPLE ERAS

Star Wars – A Long Time Ago... Screams in the Void (Vol.4)
SPAN MULTIPLE ERAS

Star Wars – A Long Time Ago... Fool's Bounty (Vol. 5)
SPAN MULTIPLE ERAS

Star Wars – A Long Time Ago... Wookiee World (Vol. 6)
SPAN MULTIPLE ERAS

Star Wars – A Long Time Ago... Far, Far Away (Vol. 7)
SPAN MULTIPLE ERAS

Star Wars Tales Vol. 1
SPAN MULTIPLE ERAS

Star Wars Tales Vol. 2
SPAN MULTIPLE ERAS

Star Wars Tales Vol. 3
SPAN MULTIPLE ERAS